Princeton Theological Monograph Series

Dikran Y. Hadidian

General Editor

8

THE WAY OF THEOLOGY IN KARL BARTH

Essays and Comments

THE WAY OF
THEOLOGY
IN
KARL BARTH

Essays and Comments

Edited by
H. Martin Rumscheidt

With an Introduction by
Stephen W. Sykes

PICKWICK PUBLICATIONS
An imprint of *Wipf and Stock Publishers*
199 West 8th Avenue • Eugene OR 97401

Pickwick Publications
An imprint of Wipf and Stock Publishers
199 W 8th Ave, Suite 3
Eugene, OR 97401

The Way of Theology in Karl Barth
Essays and Comments
Edited by Rumscheidt, H. Martin
Copyright©1986 Pickwick
ISBN: 0-915138-61-1
Publication date 1/1/1986

Contents

Foreword - **H. Martin Rumscheidt** VII

Introduction - **Stephen W. Sykes** 1

Karl Barth

    Fate and Idea in Theology 25

    The First Commandment as an Axiom of Theology 63

    Philosophy and Theology 79

FOREWORD

In 1923, Karl Barth and Adolf von Harnack, one of Barth's teachers, were engaged in an incisive public debate; it took place in the pages of the periodical *Christliche Welt*. In one of the pieces Barth contributed to that debate he wrote the following: "It is my private view that the exercise of repristinating a classical theological train of thought, which in the days of medieval and Protestant scholasticism was known as 'theology', is probably more instructive than the chaotic business of today's faculties for which the idea of a determinative *object* has become strange and monstrous in face of the determinative character of the *method*. But I also think I know that this same kind of thing can and should not return and that we must think *in* our time *for* our time. Actually the point is not to keep the historical-critical method of biblical and historical research developed in the last centuries away from the work of theology, but rather to fit that method, and its refinement of the way questions are asked, into that work in a meaningful way."[1] The issue which stood before Harnack and Barth was the interpretation of what was God's revelation and what, given that revelation, theology was as a human, scholarly discipline. Harnack represented the apex of a century-old tradition which had struggled for the veracity of theology as a serious scholarly activity and its acceptability in the academy. Barth was one of the ablest people at that time who argued that "this particular (sc. academically respected) theology might have moved further away from its theme than is good,"[2] that the preoccupation with working in terms of methods which are honored - justifiably so, one needs to add - in the academy, had shifted the priority of the theological enterprise from the ontic to the noetic, from the substance of the theological pursuit to its methodology. As a result, God, the substance or subject of theology, was ultimately thought of as really being spoken of when we humans speak loud enough of ourselves and our epistemologies.

It is manifestly unusual, given Barth's methodic self-distancing from methodological pursuits like those of Europe's and North-America's theological faculties over the last half century, to collect essays of his, provide them with an introduction and entitle the study "The Way of Theology for Karl Barth." Why was that task undertaken at all? While working on his dissertation, the editor was referred to the essay *Schicksal und Idee in der Theologie* by his *Doktorvater*, Joseph C. McLelland, and told that it would be good if that essay were some day translated into English; philosophers of religion and philosophical theologians would welcome it, he said, since the essay yielded not only such a rich insight into Barth's thinking at a crucial phase but also provided a very useful tool for comprehending the methodological diversity of recent theology. McLelland's fascination with the 'cohabitation' of philosophy and theology in the Barth-family (Karl and his brother Heinrich taught theology and philosophy - in separate faculties: - for many years at the same university in Switzerland) led him to the exploration of the 'family-affair' to which Stephen Sykes refers in his Introduction; hence his interest in the essay *Theologie und Philosophie*, written thirty years later than the essay already cited. The editor has now settled a nearly twenty year old 'debt' to an influential teacher by providing, in cooperation with the colleagues named at the end of this foreword, English translations of those two essays.

A different reason exists for making *Das erste Gebot als theologisches Axiom* available in translation, a reason which is also more directly related to the publication of the *collection* of these essays itself. To a growing number of observers the theological critique of Liberal Protestant theology by Barth is becoming a useful chart at a time when in the Anglo-Saxon world the Liberal theological tradition is both waning and less and less resourceful in face of certain pressures. Even if one is fully cognizant of the fact that no period of history in one place is ever congruent with another period somewhere else. Barth's *theological* stance in the first few years of the thirties in this century is very constructive for the theological stance vis-à-vis what is happening theologically and politically in the eighties of that same century. His call for a theology, some have called it a 'reveille', which resolutely seeks to wait upon the God to whom the Bible testifies and to wait without idols, is not only salutary for people's theological existence today but also instructive for the way in which theology is done by them, for their theological method, if the God with whom that theology seeks to occupy itself is the God to whom all honor, glory and majesty, that is all authority and power, are due, if it is the God who declares "I tolerate no other gods beside me."

Each of the three essays shows, in its own way, that the way of theology for Karl Barth was one on which that God's lordship, witnessed to and spoken of in a great variety of ways in the Bible, is of priority ontic-ly *and* noeticly. Clarity of priorities is to be valued in itself, yet it cannot singlehandedly provide the critical leverage for theological repentance and conversion or for what Barth in 1937 once called 'political worship of God,' the service of God done in political ways, on the condition that it is *God* who is followed in that worship. Barth set out to develop a theology in which that priority was fully and consistently operative. And it is that methodology which these three essays depict out of a variety of contexts in Barth's life. The people associated with the production of this book believe that a theology of such a methodological orientation is worth engaging and developing again *in* our time *for* our time.

It is the occasion of the centenary of Karl Barth's birth on May 10, 1886 which sees the completion of the task which was undertaken, with love, patience, toil and renewed respect for the depths of Barth's own work, by Dikran Y. Hadidian, the Director of Pickwick Publications, Stephen W. Sykes, Regius Professor of Divinity at Cambridge University, and the translators: George Hunsinger of Bangor, Maine, David Lochhead of Vancouver, British Columbia, Robert Palma of Holland, Michigan and the editor. To them and to Nancy Price of Cape Breton, who assisted in copy-editing, thanks and more thanks.

The editor expresses appreciation to TVZ Verlag, Zürich and the Karl Barth Archives in Basel for their agreement to have these essays published in English.

Finally, as a sign of recognition and gesture of ongoing appreciation for his persistence in pursuing his theological, ethical and political priorities, this book is dedicated to our friend 'Paulus': the Reverend Professor Paul Lehmann of New York.

Halifax, Nova Scotia　　　　　　　　　　　　　　　　*Martin Rumscheidt*
May 10, 1986

Notes

1. H. Martin Rumscheidt, *Revelation and Theology; An Analysis of the Barth-Harnack Correspondence of 1923;* Cambridge: Cambridge University Press, 1972; p.41-2.

2. *ibid.;* p. 31.

INTRODUCTION

S. W. Sykes
Regius Professor of Divinity
University of Cambridge

A number of different motivations may draw English-speaking readers to these newly-translated essays of Karl Barth on the relations of theology and philosophy. There will certainly be some whose major interest will be in Barth himself, and in the light which these essays throw upon his intellectual development and dominant theological characteristics. Others, on the other hand, may consult these pieces out of concern for the issue itself; how to locate the differing tasks of philosophers and theologians in respect to each other has been a topic of perennial controversial potential from the days of Christian Platonists of Alexandria onwards. In this introduction I propose to address myself to both of these two concerns. The essays need to be placed in an historical context (section II), and require some interpretation (section III). But my first task is to help the reader with the simple question, which of the essays to read first, by giving a brief account of their respective contents (section I).

I

The longest of the three essays, *Fate and Idea in Theology* (1929), addresses itself to the conventional distinction in intellectual history between "realism" and "idealism". Barth asks how theology, which he defines as "a technically ordered investigation into the truth about God as the object of ecclesiastical proclamation" (p. 30), is involved in this divide. Theology, he says, is related to the church as its "sphere of life" (*Lebensbereich*) in the way medicine is related to physiology. (We are here reminded inevitably of the Wittgensteinian notions of a "form of life" and a "language game"; see below, p. 20, for further discussion of this problem). God is the content of the church's sphere of life, and theology is possible only to the extent that God makes himself accessible in it. Yet theology is a human and technical discipline, working within the ordinary framework of thought and speech as discussed in philosophy. So theology has no unambiguous categories at its disposal. There are no guaranteed ways in which it can demonstrate that God is really being spoken of in this human language. If genuine speech about

God happens at all, it is a miracle of grace; and the theologian is constantly exposed to the temptation of turning herself or himself into a philosopher, a betrayal which can occur either openly and consciously, or covertly and unintentionally.

The point Barth is striving to make is the need for incessant watchfulness, because the human discipline of theology is a reflection upon reality by means of the very same thought which is also the tool of the philosophers. The basic problem of all philosophy, the very same realist idealist divide, will, therefore, also play a decisive role in theology. Theology too will be tempted to see God in fate (the realist option) or God in idea (the idealist option).

Barth first discusses the impact on theology of the concept of fate (*Schicksal*). What Barth gathers together under this term is at first sight bewilderingly various. The philosophical theology of Thomas Aquinas, Spinoza's identification of God and nature, and Schleiermacher's doctrine of absolute dependence are each at different stages deployed as examples of "realism". To hear what Barth has to say we must evidently abandon some preconceived ideas about the history of philosophy, together with Coleridge's division of thinkers into Aristotelians and Platonists.[1] The "realism" which Barth has in mind is evidently a form of empiricism which discovers God in the fate which befalls humankind *either* outwardly *or* inwardly, or in a combination of both, a fate which becomes too powerful for them, setting them in a situation of absolute dependence.

On such a definition Barth is able to embrace the sort of empiricism which insists on an analogy between the being of God and that of humanity (the so-called *analogia entis*) and also the experiential theology of the subjective consciousness. Both objectivism and subjectivism are ready to talk of God as given in experience; and, says Barth, there are important elements of truth in this view. In this sense he is quite ready to say that the theologian must be more realist than idealist. That God is revealed in Christ by the Holy Spirit is the affirmation of a true theology, emphasising at once the objective and subjective sides of revelation. But there is a crucial distinction between speaking of God as an actuality, and lapsing into the God-as-fate temptation. This difference is only revealed when certain questions are honestly faced. For example, "does revelation really do no more than confirm and reinforce supernaturally a naively presupposed human capacity and necessity apparently somehow given with our experience as such" (p. 42). Is God's address something genuinely new, encountering human beings as sinners? Is God's reality that of an agent, not just of a kind of givenness? Is there an underside of dread before the fact that God hides himself in his revelation? We can, says Barth, only ask, so as to be alert to the dangers.

The concept of idea (*Idee*), the second of the pair in order of logical priority, can likewise not be set aside without more ado. Critical reflection about truth reveals the weakness of naive realism, as did Platonism, nominalism, Descartes and Kant in the history of philosophy. No theology, he avers, "has ever avoided the general problem of idealism" (p. 47); indeed sophisticated theology, such as Thomism, has a proper idealist dimension. One must not damn theologies by pointing to the realist or idealist philosophical influences which have played upon them. Christian idealism, for all its tendency towards mysticism, is certainly possible.

Despite all this, critical objections must also be lodged. Barth is notably more severe with idealism because of its ever-present temptation of qualifying or even denying that theology has fundamentally to do with God's access to us, not our access to God. The transcendence of God is something more than and different from human self-transcendence. Theology is not the production of truth, but bearing witness to it. Truth is substantiated by God's action alone, not by human collaborative work. The activity of reason is fundamentally guided and ordered by something superior to itself, a matter of command and obedience.

Barth concludes his essay by arguing against the possibility of including both realist and idealist poles in a synthetic whole. Proper theology has to think dialectically and eschew the dubious benefits of systematization. Why so? The reason Barth gives is that theology must be done in the acknowledgement of the contradiction in human existence. God cannot be discovered by human self-reflection; that would be to turn theology into anthropology. But there is an unavoidable either/or to be confronted in God as he is actually given to us. Not to acknowledge this is to fall again into that theology of glory against which Luther warned. We have to pursue the hazardous task of conceptualizing God, by the use of dialectical opposites, without practising the art of synthesis. Faced with the sophisticated theologies of the past like those of Thomas Aquinas or Schleiermacher we must raise questions, as our only defence against degeneration. Only in this way can we preserve the possibility that the knowledge of God comes through to us. "Theological reality, in our case and theirs, might always be as mixed and ambiguous as reality in general" (p. 61).

Theological schemes must be conscious of their own relativity to the truth of God's free divine election. Theology must always ask itself whether its concept of God is a witness to God. Thus theologians must be prepared to value again, as did the old Reformed dogmaticians, the doctrine of predestination and to begin its work with a human affirmation of God's free grace in Jesus Christ.

The slighter and more rhetorical piece, *The First Commandment as an Axiom of Theology* (1933), argues that all theology is founded on an axiom, that is "a statement which is sufficiently comprehensive and substantial to form the ultimate and decisive presupposition to the proof of all other statements of a particular scientific discipline" (p. 66). But having borrowed this term from logic, Barth promptly insists that an axiom *in theology* must be *sui generis*; that in order to say what needs to be uttered the concept of axiom will have to be *mis*used. It would even be wrong to speak of an "analogous" use (i.e. a combination of similarities and differences), unless one says that the concept receives its appropriateness by the likeness conferred on it by faith (here Barth cites Romans 12:6). Thus "whatever 'axiom' means here must be determined by the matter which it designates in this discussion irrespective of the general sense of that concept" (p. 67).

Specifically in theology, then, the axiom signifies a written commandment to which the church is always obedient, a report concerning an event in time and history, and as a command of the liberating and saving God to be obeyed in thankfulness. The proper theological understanding of an axiom is always to be distinguished as an event of grace from any idea of "orders of creation" (Barth is here distancing himself from the work of his Swiss contemporary, Emil Brunner; see below, (p. 17 - 18).

The first commandment is the axiom of theology in that it forbids the possession of other gods before the Lord. Barth follows Luther's exposition of this commandment in insisting that there is a plurality of possible gods, some of whom may be confused with the true God. To cling solely to the God who is merciful in Jesus Christ appears to be a disastrous narrowness of horizon, a negativity towards other values, and a restriction of the possible sources of theology. Recent Protestantism has specialized in adding to revelation with the word "and" a variety of attractive candidates (revelation "and" religious consciousness, culture, the history of religion, creation or primordial revelation, human existence and so forth).

But one must ask questions of this tendency. Has it transferred its zeal and passion to the second term in the pair? Is it aware of danger of an alien framework, of the control of revelation by reason? Is it clear that there can be no intermixing, exchange or identification of the content of the two terms.

Contemporary theology must have the confidence to take leave of natural theology as did the reformers. The both/and of catholic theology, with its impressive roots in the Augustinian-Thomistic tradition must be radically challenged, together with its feeble variant in modern Protestantism's receptiveness to natural theology. Why? "Because everything else is arbitrariness which does not lead to, but leads away from that god (sc. who has revealed himself in Jesus Christ)" (p. 80). There can be no final resolution of this radical movement of obedience. Barth again emphasises that one can only ask questions, and at the same time allow one's own theology to be open to the same enquiry. "The necessary fight of theology can be fought properly only in a common hope" (p. 81).

Our final essay, "Philosophy and Theology" (1960), contributed to his younger brother, Heinrich's, seventieth birthday *Festschrift* is a calmer, but not for that reason in any sense more conciliatory piece. Barth expresses himself doubtful of the wisdom of juxtaposing and contrasting philosophy and theology in the abstract. Nonetheless he sees the respective tasks of philosophers and theologians as heading in opposite directions. Though both are concerned with one single truth, and both work on human endeavours, nonetheless their tasks are not in any straightforward sense analogous, and there is a clear difference in the order of the "components of the one whole truth" which confronts them both. The theologian works in a descending order, from the living creator to the creature; the philosopher, exactly the reverse. There cannot therefore be a "Christian philosophy" which is both properly philosophy and also Christian. Barth expresses himself reluctant to prescribe for philosophers the nature of their own discipline, but he anticipates that, on this account of theology, philosophers will have little but distant amazement for theology. With constant reference to the influential piece by Kant on the *Dispute between the Faculties*,[2] Barth cannot envisage anything other than conflict between faithful theologians and genuine philosophers, in which, from the theological side at least, concessions are out of order. The path of Jesus Christ, which the theologian confesses without shame at its naïvité, is from above to below and from there back again.

The only concessions to coexistence which Barth feels able to add at the close of his essay are to the effect that philosophers and theologians ought to remain within earshot of each other, and that they are both capable of learning from each other. But what could philosophers possibly learn from theologians? Barth declines to give a straight answer from the side of theology, ironically suggesting that in their heart of hearts theologians believe that the history of philosophy, apart from formal logic, has come to an end. And what could theologians learn from philosophy? Barth believes that genuine progress can be made from the creaturely point of view, despite the fact that in the end of the day it must be regarded as flawed. Some theologians evidently think too little about human existence, their primary task making them careless about their secondary task. Good philosophy may challenge this, but at the same time may tempt theologians to become cryptophilosophers and pseudo-theologians. Good theology would in effect be "theanthropology".

Barth plainly does not expect philosophers to capitulate to this prescription of a subordinate role, and consequently anticipates a prolonged, and good-tempered, co-existence in hope. He reminds his younger brother of their father's deployment of Psalm 133:1, "Behold, how good it is, and how pleasant, when brothers live together in unity".

II

"If we open our mouths, we find ourselves in the province of philosophy".[3] Barth's realisation of the inescapability of clarifying his relationship with the claims of philosophy is rooted in his earliest encounters with German philosophy and philosophy of religion as a student. Reared as all German theologians were upon the careful study of Kant and Schleiermacher, and sharing in his student days in the heated discussion of the radical proposals of Ernst Troeltsch, Barth was nonetheless most deeply endebted to the Marburg theologian, Wilhelm Herrmann (1846-1922).[4] In 1925, partly on the basis of lecture notes taken as a student, Barth presented the heart of Herrmann's position, a sustained attempt to do justice to the autonomy of Christian dogmatics and to protect it from "intellectualism".[5] This threat Herrmann believed he saw in four theological misunderstandings, the attempt to prove God's existence, the depiction of religion as the deepest motive of the spiritual life of humanity, the Kantian reduction of religion to moral earnestness, and the definition of religion as the feeling of absolute dependence (Schleiermacher). The common element of all these is the reduction of religion to something else entailing its explicability at the bar of reason.

In an entirely general sense Barth's entire theological programme can be seen as the attempt to do justice to the autonomy of Christian dogmatics, to listen to the Divine Word, and to be obedient to what God alone, in his sovereign freedom, makes possible by his self-revelation. Necessarily, the pretensions of the unaided human intellect are identified as a major source of corruption and enslavement. Necessarily, too, the dominance of liberal progressive opinion in the tradition of the "father of modern theology", Friedrich Schleiermacher, had to be challenged. Nonetheless it is one of the ironies of the history of theology that for Schleiermacher himself, the major task was to free theology from its philosophical entrapment. This in part explains Barth's curiously ambivalent relationship to Schleiermacher, which still awaits a fully satisfactory treatment. On the one hand at an early stage Barth dethrones Schleiermacher from the company of those whom he would regard as authentic theologians,[6] and consciously presents his own developing programme for a Dogmatics as a "counterachievement";[7] on the other hand, he is much more deeply respectful of Schleiermacher's work than of many of his liberal protestant successors and at the very end of his life indicated his abiding openness of mind on the question of how Schleiermacher is to be understood.[8]

After his student days Barth served from 1911-1921 as a pastor in a growing agricultural and industrial village in the Aargau, Switzerland. Here, largely through an orientation towards religious socialism, he began to make a series of friendships of paramount importance to his future career. Eduard Thurneysen, whom he had already known as a student, came in 1914 to be pastor of a nearby village.[9] Emil Brunner from Zürich he met at a Religious Socialist conference in Aarau. And when, after the war, Swiss Religious Socialism began to be of interest in Germany, Barth encountered Friedrich Gogarten at a conference in Tambach, Thuringia at which he gave a notable paper, "The Christian's Place in Society" (1919).[10]

But the achievement which catapulted Barth from the pastoral into the academic sphere was the writing of his commentary on the *Epistle to the Romans* (first edition, 1919; second edition, 1922). Initially known only in Switzerland, the wider circulation of this vigorous work was apparently the cause of his being invited to a chair of Reformed Theology at Göttingen. The success of this appointment, which he took up in 1921, was greatly assisted by the remarkable reception accorded the second edition of *Romans*. Though assailed by many as unscientific, one expert reviewer, Rudolf Bultmann, showed real understanding of Barth's programme of theological exegesis.[11] The movement of theology to which Barth had given a new voice and a new prominence in due time gave birth to its own journal, *Zwischen den Zeiten* (Between the Times), founded by Barth, Brunner and Gogarten, and devoted to the development of a theology of the word in opposition to that of Liberal Protestantism.

The writings of this period give clear notice of the theme which is subsequently worked up in the present writings on philosophy and theology. It is, for Barth, of paramount importance that a distinction be made between God and the world, and that Christians be open to the fact that God has let himself be known as God, before rushing to speak of religion, morality and culture.[12] Barth does not see this separation as a matter of flight from the world. He refers at this point to biblical eschatology, of such importance to exegetes of the time. Eschatology means, he says, genuine hope for humanity and for the physical side of human life, in the victory of Jesus Christ over death.[13] Everything, then, turns on the movement of God in history, "a new compulsion from above", and it is this movement which we must strive to understand.[14]

> To understand! Let me compress into one word the meaning of our part in this unbroken movement of life into death and out of death into life: to understand! We must understand the mighty God-given restlessness of man and by it the mighty shaking of the foundations of the world... To understand means to have the insight of God that all of this must be just as it is and not otherwise. To understand means to take the whole situation upon us in the fear of God, and in the fear of God to enter into the movement of the era. To understand means to be given in order to give.[15]

Later Barth was to take the aphorism *fides quaerens intellectum* (Faith seeking Understanding)[16] from Anselm as a token of the consistency with which he proposed to construe the irreversible movement from God to humanity. But in the middle phase of his work, the so-called dialectical period (1919-27), he was ready to lay strong emphasis, as we have seen, on the phenomenon of human restlessness (with reference especially to Kierkegaard) as a sign of the human need of God. In a speech of 1922 the way of dialectic is contrasted both with that of dogmatism and of the mystical *via negativa*.[17] It is dialectic which alone understands *both* the obligation *and* impossibility of speaking of God.

Two further elements in the preparation of Barth's mature position are of importance, the treatment of Feuerbach and the intensive encounter with Roman Catholic theology. In the works of the philosopher, Ludwig Feuerbach (1804-1874), Barth believes that he saw the kind of inevitable reduction to which the theology of the early nineteenth century had exposed itself. When Feuerbach asserted that "theology long ago became anthropology" could he really be blamed, Barth asks?[18] The whole tendency of theology from Pietism to the Enlightenment and into the Romantic movement had "let itself be driven by the upsurge of a self-glorifying and self-satisfied humanism". Feuerbach's question to modern theology ought to stop contemporary theology in its tracks, and force upon it the question whether God is truly given in the religious consciousness of humanity. It remained axiomatic for Barth that "theology is in no sense to be anthropology" (see below, p. 58). It is interesting to note that in a 1927 article on Feuerbach Barth regards Feuerbach's attention to Luther's doctrine of faith and emphasis on the properties of the deity to the humanity of Christ as a signal advertising a danger implicit in Luther and Lutheranism,[19] into which he already believed that his friend and collaborator, Friedrich Gogarten, had fallen.[20]

That Barth had turned away from the fashionable Liberal Protestantism of his youth to the study and exposition of the Reformers was already obvious in lectures he gave at Göttingen in 1922 and 1923 on Calvin and on Zwingli. "Only now," he wrote subsequently, "were my eyes properly open to the reformers". More surprisingly, and scarcely less important, was his induction into the thought of St Thomas Aquinas, first in lectures from the young Erik Peterson in 1923-24 (later to become a Roman Catholic in 1930),[21] and subsequently on his removal to Münster in 1925 in interaction with members of the larger and older Roman Catholic faculty of Theology.[22] The conviction grew in him that in the Roman Catholic Church the substance of theology had been better preserved than in modern Protestantism, and in two seminars, on St Anselm's *Cur Deus Homo* (1926), and on St Thomas *Summa* Book I (1928-29), he made strenuous efforts to grasp the Roman Catholic position on the relation of philosophy and theology.

The positive character of his response to aspects of St Thomas is clear from the essay *Fate and Idea in Theology* (see especially pp. 31, 37, 38, 39 and 42 below). What is also clear is his rejection of what he calls the *analogia entis* (the analogy of being). This is an elusive concept and still the subject of considerable debate. But according to Barth in 1929,

> *analogia entis* means that every existing being and we as human beings participate in the *similitudo Dei* (likeness to God). The experience of God becomes an inherent possibility and necessity (p. 42 - 43).

Against this Barth holds that the capacity for experiencing God cannot be regarded as something natural. Grace is always an event, not an inherent capacity. What Barth feared in the *analogia entis* was a conceptual scheme, founded on the notion of being, which would link God and humanity in a single philosophical structure.

Barth inferred that this was *the* principle of Roman Catholicism ("I regard the *analogia entis* as the invention of Antichrist", *Church Dogmatics I/I* 1923, ET by G.W. Bromiley 1975, p. xiii) from his encounters with the writings and person of a vigorous Jesuit, Erich Przywara, who had already responded to Barth's work in 1923 and 1924, had been invited by Barth to the seminar on St Thomas' *Summa*.[23] At this time Roman Catholic theologians were in reaction against an earlier stress on the supernatural, and in the work of Karl Adam and Przywara efforts were made to present an organic relationship between natural and supernatural. It was for this reason that Barth was able to draw parallels between what he depicted as standard Roman Catholicism and tendencies in Liberal Protestantism. In fact there were other important Roman Catholic voices who made clear that Catholic thought also knew of an analogy *of faith*, the term Barth had opposed to analogy of being.[24] Barth acknowledged this in 1940, but expressed doubt whether this was in any sense the official position.[25] Barth also recognised that it was not true that St Thomas Aquinas had synthesised God and the creaturely world in a concept of being, since *Deus non est in aliquo genere* (God is not in any class or kind, citing the *Summa theologiae* I, 3, 5).[26] Not until the perceptive work of Hans Urs von Balthasar in 1951 was the discussion raised to a new clarity,[27] and it is to be noted that the complex question of how Barth's understanding of the analogy of faith is to be understood in relation to creation and human being is by no means closed.[28] The reader of these essays must be warned, at least, that Barth's engagement with Roman Catholic attempts to relate philosophy and theology are at a relatively primitive stage, and no over-simplified conclusions can or should be drawn from them.[29]

If a question mark necessarily hangs over Barth's depiction of what he rejects, it is plain enough what he has embraced. Especially is this the case in his positive, but never uncritical reception to the thought of Luther. It was Barth himself who depicted the change between the two editions of his commentary on the Romans as a move from Osiander to Luther.[30] And it is no surprise to find that in the winter of 1932-33 (when Barth was teaching in Bonn) the text for a discussion group was Luther's *Greater Catechism*, from which derives a vital quotation commenting on the first commandment (see below, p.72). From Luther plainly Barth derives his often repeated stress on divine election, on the irreversible order of God's act from God to humanity, on opposition to all hint of a theology of glory, on justification by faith alone, and on the perversity of the human will. As we have seen Barth is also capable, as a good Calvinist, of perceiving weaknesses in Luther, and their fruit in his Lutheran collaborators. Rudolf Bultmann he was already regarding with some suspicion as early as 1925 for thinking in terms which he described as "too anthropological - Kierkegaardian - Lutheran (and Gogartenian)".[31] The dialogue with Bultmann continued in 1928 when Bultmann charged Barth with culpable failure in his work, to take philosophy seriously, *Prolegomena zur Christlichen Dogmatik* (1928).[32] By pretending to ignore philosophy Barth, he claims, has fallen prey to an outdated philosophy. Bultmann agrees that a systematic philosophy is a peril to a dogmatics. But dogmatics, he is persuaded, actually *requires* the analysis of the situation of the believer provided only by an existential-ontological philosophy. Only under such conditions can philosophy genuinely be a handmaid, not a mistress, of theology.

> Your planned ignoring of philosophy is only apparent. Naturally lordship or servanthood applies to the forming of concepts. But if dogmatics is to be a science, it cannot avoid the question of appropriate concepts.[33]

In his reply, four days later, Barth admits that he is no philosopher, and that he is repelled by the spectacle of theology adjusting itself to the philosophy of its age. But he claims that more than one professional philosopher has seen what he is trying to do (he does not say which, though Heinrich Scholz may have been among them.), in his somewhat eclectic and dilettante use of philosophical concepts.[34] But he begs to doubt whether anything would be advanced by his spending the rest of his life acquiring an unambiguous philosophical terminology from the phenomenologists to deploy in his description of the human situation.

This exchange of letters clarifies the concerns which Barth has in his essay, *Fate and Idea in Theology* (1929). Here he makes a sustained attempt both to meet the challenge of Bultmann to take philosophy seriously and also to avoid the specious attractions of sophisticated Thomism. Barth presents himself, in philosophical terms, as a critical realist, that is to say one who primarily is concerned with actuality and occurrence, but who acknowledges the necessity of attending to the conditions and limitations of human knowing. Even when it is faithfully about its own business theology cannot escape the problem of philosophy (see below, p. 56).

At this point it becomes necessary to say a word about a concept which figures prominently in all Barth's writings of the 1920's, that of dialectic. This is a word with a host of subtly different meanings, which Barth deploys in contexts where he wishes to advertise the fact that we are in the presence of unassimilable opposites. Barth compares the method of dialectic to walking along a narrow ridge looking from one side to the other, from positive to negative, and negative to positive.[35] This is the only way in which one may speak of God at all, by the insight that "God (but really God!) becomes man (but really man!)".[36] Plainly there was in the dialectical programme the possibility of giving, consistently with Reformation dogmatics, a realistic or pessimistic account of the human person. Bultmann's attempt to persuade Barth that Heideggerian existentialism supplied this lack seems to have been counterproductive. Instead of incorporating a consistent philosophical ontology, Barth moved, through his further consideration of analogy in his book on St Anselm of Canterbury, *Fides Quaerens Intellectum*, to subordinate dialectic to the thought that God and humanity share a common narrative, God's own story. Barth is advertising his decisive turn away from existentialism when he writes (in 1929):

> Theology thinks dialectically, because this contradiction (sc. between realism and idealism) has been placed into the world of thought and existence by God's word, as something it and only it resolves (p. 58 below).

The Anselm book provided the ground-work for the more rigorous execution of the methodology which Barth had espoused all along. Claiming that he had previously been hindered by "the eggshells of a philosophical system",[37] he now proposed to be more directly and plainly receptive to Calvin as distinct from Luther, and advertised his rejection of Bultmann in the revised Dogmatics by quoting a remark of his brother, Heinrich:

> That theology should begin with a definition of existence, or man. . . is at root a piece of Liberalism.[38]

The new rigour of his approach is evident in his response to Brunner's, *Das Gebot und die Ordnungen* (1932)[39] and *Die Frage nach dem "Anknüpfungspunkt" als Problem der Theologie*.[40] In the former of these works, which Barth studied as soon as it appeared, there are some observations of a mildly critical nature on Barth's alleged failure to develop an adequate doctrine of creation and his neglect of the early chapters of Calvin's *Institutes* which speak of humanity's knowledge of the creator.[41] Barth's response was immediate and negative. From our vantage point it must be remembered that 1933 was the year of the Nazi seizure of power. Barth's instinctive and immediate rejection of Nazi ideology was the rejection of a false god. But to his horror he realised that Protestantism in Germany, so frequently compromised in the past with false philosophies, lacked the clarity of insight to enable it to resist the new threat of assimilation. Gogarten, whom he had long regarded with suspicion, briefly appeared among the German Christians. Brunner's work, which under other circumstances he might have regarded with more tolerance, seemed to be yet another dangerous compromise with natural theology. The lecture containing a reply to Brunner, *The First Commandment as a Theological Axiom*, was delivered in Copenhagen and Aarhus in Denmark within two weeks of the Reichstag fire.[42] The same charge that had earlier been levelled at Bultmann was now aimed as his colleague, Brunner. He too was identified as standing within the compromised heritage of Schleiermacher (below, p. 79). The precise offence was Brunner's doctrine of "orders of creation", and his insistence on a "point of contact" between God and humanity in the divinely created orders. In the following year Brunner defined the position which he proposed to maintain against Barth in the following way:

> The Word of God could not reach a man who had lost his consciousness of God entirely. A man without conscience cannot be struck by the call, "Repent ye and believe the Gospel." What the natural man knows of God, of the law and of his own dependence upon God, may be very confused and distorted. But even so it is the necessary, indispensable point of contact for divine grace.[43]

Barth's angry rejoinder, No!, beginning with the celebrated words (remarkably like those of Professor Higgins in *My Fair Lady*) "I am by nature a gentle being and entirely averse to all unnecessary disputes", is well known.[44] Later Barth was to excuse the violence of his reply by claiming that Brunner had no understanding of the German Church conflict and thus no feel for the human and political context of the argument.[45] Brunner subsequently remarked with some satisfaction that

The Divine Imperative had been recognised by National Socialists in Germany as anti-totalitarian, and accordingly confiscated and destroyed.[46]

Further rupture occurred in his relationship with his brother Heinrich, on Barth's own open admission.[47] Here the reasons are shadowy; Karl increasingly found his brother's position to be opposed to his own; Heinrich evidently found Karl impossibly self-opinionated.[48] Recently an attempt has been made to demonstrate that Heinrich's views are in "large accord" with those of Barth, and that both operate within a Kantian problematic.[49] The essay printed in this volume is in no very obvious sense a "reply" or even a "response" to Heinrich's philosophical labours. What is significant, however, is its overt references to Kant's *Dispute of the Faculties*.[50] In this work Kant had portrayed with considerable irony the necessary conflict which exists between the freedom of philosophy and the confessional (ultimately constitutional) conformity of theology. This "unavoidable conflict" Barth seems to accept. Philosophers, he believes, will not be likely to abandon their characteristic point of departure which is opposed to that of the faithful theologian. For their part theologians, while not wishing to dictate what philosophers ought to learn from theology, might, nonetheless, were they to "open their gloomy hearts", issue "the impudent and untenable demand" that philosophers recognize that their discipline had come to an end, and that all that was left was the history of philosophy and formal logic (see below, pp.95). It is characteristic of Barth, and only partly disarming, that so stark a view, which is certainly his own, should be uttered in this ironic self-distancing tone.[51] But at this point the substantive issue becomes unavoidable. Can the terms on which Barth distinguishes the tasks of philosophy and theology be taken seriously today?

III

It should be remembered, in the first place, that Barth never denies that theology is *human* speech of God. There is no pure, philosophically uncontaminated exegesis of Scripture. Barth has a potent sentence in *Fate and Idea* about the absurdity of trying to discredit the thought of one's theological opponent "by pointing to the realist or idealist philosopher who stands in the wings". Even more pungently in the *Church Dogmatics* (I/2, of 1939) he remarks on the "grotesque comedy" of imagining that whereas others have fallen victim to this or that philosophy, one has oneself merely abided wholly by the facts.[52] Against such delusions Barth advances the inevitability, but provisionality of all philosophical approaches to Scripture. Philosophy is only a danger to exegesis if it is incapable of being criticised by what is read in the text.[53] From this follows Barth's use of the interrogative method, already evident in the present essays. One can, says Barth, only ask. Human language itself contains the seeds of an inevitable degeneration.

> When it comes to others - whether a Thomas or a Schleiermacher or a Biedermann - we can do no more than raise questions. What do we really know? What do we know even when it comes to the philosophers? Do we really know whether they are chasing after the phantasm of a "naked God" (*Deus nudus*) attained by "rational investigation" (*judicio rationis*)? Do we really know whether their thinking merely heads towards the point from which we believe ours must set forth, whether theirs is not at least as good if not better than our own? Is it clear to us how easily we ourselves can be caught in the act of not setting forth from that point? (see below, p. 61).

The interrogative must be seen as embracing the dogmatic. It is relatively easy to catch Barth in the act of making a sweeping claim on epistemological grounds - understand things my way, or not at all. Many imitators, and critics, of Barth see in him nothing other than a theological dogmatist given to the assertion that the standpoint occupied by the Christian theologian is inherently epistemologically privileged. If, as I am suggesting, the interrogative embraces the dogmatic, then the position has to be qualified. It remains the case that a theological position can and must be asserted on the basis of the claim that it follows the pattern of God's own dealings with humanity. But the mere *fact* of making the claim guarantees nothing, to claimant or to anyone exposed to it. It is advanced, as Barth says in the *Church Dogmatics*, as a piece of counsel, not as a binding law.[54] Barth is under no illusion that others may think differently. But it does not follow from the mere fact of diversity of view that a presumption is established against anyone who makes a serious claim, nor against the corollary that so serious a claim must be advanced with conviction. The soggy pluralism and relativism exhibited by liberal theologies is, according to Barth, their own refutation.

The ambiguity of the relationship between the interrogative and the dogmatic makes it the more intelligible why Barth's account of the relations of theology with philosophy has precisely led in subsequent theology to a form of aesthetic relativism. Barth's contention that theology is necessarily a Church discipline, by which what is being proclaimed by the Church in word and deed is subjected to critical scrutiny in the light of the Word of God, when taken together with certain suggestions of Wittgenstein about "language games", has led to the development of a view that Christian living is a discrete cultural "form of life" whose language can only be intelligibly construed on the inside. Readers of these essays will perceive at once the contradiction between this position and Barth's view that there is *one* truth which confronts and claims philosophers and theologians *qua* human beings.

A variant of the same relativistic tendency has seized upon the narrative turn in Barth's account of the act of God to present a perspectival "theology of story", according to which each person makes up for themselves their own story-meaning and relates this in some way to the narrative of the church. Again it will be obvious to any student of these essays that Barth's criticism of the greater dangers of idealism encompasses both cruder and more refined versions of such self-indulgent subjectivism. Stories of this kind as readily deceive and mislead as they signify the truth. And it is no service to theology if, in gratefully accepting Barth's contention for the separability of the tasks of theology and philosophy, theologians lapse into fashionable, but uncritical modes of apologetic.

The nub of Barth's dogmatic position and the key to understanding it is the rejection which it implies of an autonomous anthropology. The problem is encapsulated by Barth in the following way:

> Anthropology. . . is in non-theological belief, myth, philosophy and science a kind of basic discipline which imposes its criterion on all other knowledge and perhaps claims to embrace it (*Church Dogmatics* III/2, p.21).

This *imposition* and *claim to comprehensiveness* Barth proposes to frustrate by an unparalleled exercise of embattled theological consistency, which it is all too easy to misrepresent. As we have seen, Bultmann, in response to the abandoned project of a Christian dogmatics, accused Barth of stumbling into a philosophical schematism by sheer lack of attention to the problem of philosophy. Later writers have followed suit, demonstrating, to their own satisfaction at least, Barth's (concealed) philosophical commitments.

But it is plain from our exposition that Barth has already anticipated the charge by admitting that because theology shares a common language with philosophy it is necessarily open to that criticism. The criticism is, therefore, trivial unless it can also be shown in what way the philosophical language or framework has intruded upon the proper substance of theology, obedience to God's self-revelation. But if this is to be demonstrated, then that self-revelation is going to be used as a criterion for theology - in which case Barth's original position is justified. For Barth there can be no propositions of an autonomous anthropology which are more certain than the truth of God's word.

Let us make one point in favour of Barth's argument here, and one point against it. In favour is the fundamentally critical and interrogative character of what Barth proposes. This is the reason why in the Anglo-Saxon world of the late 1950's and 60's there were philosophers, bred in a strongly positivist, anti-idealist atmosphere, who warmly welcomed Barth's realism and his refusal of the seductive attractions of speculative forms of existentialist ontology. Those who sharply distinguished between constructive or systematic metaphysics and the analytic task of a metaphysical enquiry, turned to Barth as an ally for the view that the major tasks of a philosopher of religion were critical rather than speculative.[55] And there is still every reason to take seriously the proposal that theology must be constantly on guard against the unintentional subversion of its metaphors by their mere propinquity to language usages which have subtly different commitments. No one can be certain in advance that his contingency has been adequately guarded against; one can only ask, as Barth says. At root this is the position of the critical realist who asserts the irreplaceability and cognitive content of metaphorical language in both science and theology and decries the possibility of adequate "translation" into non-metaphorical speculative abstractions of philosophical origin.

Against Barth, however, one can urge the (unsurprisingly) dated quality of his attitude towards science. When he contrasts speculative philosophical anthropology (of a type undeniably more prevalent in continental Europe than in the Anglo-Saxon world of the time) with what he calls "scientific anthropology" (including psychology and sociology!), he offers the view that the latter, dealing only with the human person as a phenomenon, cannot be in opposition to Christian theological anthropology. This seems altogether too sanguine a view. The current state of argument in relation to patriarchalism and to theories of male super-ordination, prescinding from its more vapid apologetic, patently turns upon the status of the evidence from psychology, social anthropology, and sociology. On the theological side of the issue it is undeniable that the Scriptures of both Old and New Testament are permeated by patriarchial assumptions. Barth's quite sensitive, but patriarchal, discussion of the major biblical texts gives us no way of handling the charges, either that there is internal variety and inconsistency between different strands of the New Testament, or that, as a whole, the early church is seen from a relentlessly male perspective. The Barthian counter question against these observations could plainly be that the philosophy of feminism is precisely an instance of an autonomous anthropology "imposing its criterion on all other knowledge" (see above).

I have raised the issue of feminism at the close of this introduction for two reasons: First, because it is a reminder that the kind of philosophising against which Barth asserted the autonomy of theology was the kind of systematic, all-embracing world view which inevitably sees Christianity as a competitor. The Anglo-Saxon world, which for much of the twentieth century has lacked a tradition of philosophical anthropology, has now encountered in the complex, many-layered phenomenon of feminism a movement which stands in an ambiguous relationship with the Christian tradition. The questions which the liberationist movement poses for contemporary Christians, though not the same as those which Barth faced in the late 1920's and 1930's, nevertheless press with a similar kind of urgency.

The second reason for raising this issue is that it introduces more complexity into the task of exegesis than Barth was evidently willing to allow. He was, of course, familiar with the relativising impact of the history-of-religions' school of biblical scholarship, notably in the work of Ernst Troeltsch. But the questions raised by this school have not diminished in urgency. It is quite proper to ask, and to seek for an answer, whether the biblical documents themselves do not embrace and express an anthropology, rooted in the "science" of the day, which cannot constitute the sole criterion for the detection and dismissal of an alien, contemporary "philosophical" or speculative anthropology. The complexity of the status of various disciplines plainly cry out for clarification. We should at this point above all heed Barth's warning and refrain from freezing "philosophy" into an abstract definition. Theology needs for its own health vigorous combative partners, ready to challenge the terms on which theologians lay down divisions and separations so as to preserve the autonomy of their discipline. But it is still true (and for the same reason as in Barth's day, namely, because of the rapid encroachment of practical secularism upon every sphere of life), that theologians need to acquire confidence in the reality with which their discipline has to do, a confidence which needs by no means entail a loss of humility or unwillingness to learn from past mistakes.

NOTES

1. Compare the exploration of this theme by David Newsome in *Two Classes of Men, Platonism and English Romantic Thought* (London, John Murray, 1974).

2. Immanuel Kant, Der Streit der Fakultäten, In *Kant Werke*, Bd. 9 Schriften zur Anthropologie, Geschichtsphilosophie, Politik und Pädagogik (Darmstadt, Wissenschaftliche Buchgesellschaft, 1971). pp. 267-393. Translated as *Conflict of the Faculties* (The Janus Library, New York, Abaris, 1979). Compare K. -H. Crumbach, *Theologie in kritischer Öffentlichkeit*: Die Frage Kants an das Kirchliche Christentum (München, Kaiser/Grünewald, 1977).

3. Karl Barth, *Credo*, A Presentation of the Chief Problems of Dogmatics with reference to the Apostles' Creed (London, Hodder, 1936), p. 183.

4. This section is much endebted to Eberhard Busch's biographical study, *Karl Barth* (London, SCM Press, 1975). On Barth as Herrmann's pupil, see Busch esp. pp. 44-52.

5. "The Principles of Dogmatics according to Wilhelm Herrmann", in Karl Barth, *Theology and Church*, shorter writings 1920-1928 (London, SCM Press, 1962), pp. 238-271.

6. Cf. "The Word of God and the Task of the Ministry" (delivered at the meeting of the Friends of the *Christliche Welt*, 1922) in Karl Barth, *The Word of God and the Word of Man* (ET. 1928; New York, Harper Torchbook, 1957), p. 195. This lecture was regarded as marking the rebellion of a new generation against the theological liberalism represented precisely by the periodical *Christliche Welt*. See now the letters exchanged between Martin Rade, editor of the magazine, and Karl Barth, C. Schwöbel (ed), *Karl Barth - Martin Rade, Ein Briefwechsel* (Gütersloh, Gerd Mohn, 1981), esp. pp. 179-182.

7. The idea that Schleiermacher could be vanquished, not by cavilling criticism of detail, but only by a "corresponding counter-achievement", was taken from the philosophical theologian, Heinrich Scholz. In 1946 Barth was ready to say that this counter-achievement had not yet appeared; see Karl Barth, *Protestant Theology in the Nineteenth Century* (London, SCM Press, 1972), p. 427.

8. See Barth's "Nachwort" in H. Bolli (ed), *Schleiermacher - Auswahl* (München and Hamburg, Siebenstern Taschenbuch Verlag), pp. 290-312, now translated in D. Ritschl (ed), Karl Barth, *The Theology of Schleiermacher* (Edinburgh, T. and T. Clark, 1982), pp. 261-279. See also the translation of that essay, prepared by George Hunsinger: "Concluding Unscientific Postscript on Schleiermacher"in *Studies in Religion Sciences Religieuses*, Vol. 7, 1978, pp. 117-135. We should note that one of the themes of this late essay, the question of how Schleiermacher's emphasis on religious experience relates to the doctrine of the Holy Spirit, already occurs in the essay on Fate and Idea in Theology (below pp. 45).

9. See *Revolutionary Theology in the Making*, Barth-Thurneysen Correspondence, 1914-1925 (London, Epworth Press, 1964). These letters were translated by J.D. Smart, who has written an enlightening comment on their significance in H.-Martin Rumscheidt (ed), *Karl Barth in Re-view* (Pittsburgh, Pa., Pickwick Press),

pp. 55-64. Two volumes of the correspondence to 1930 are now available in the Barth *Gesamtausgabe* (V, 3 and 4).

10. Also translated in *The Word of God and the Word of Man* (footnote 6 above).

11. Barth first met Bultmann as a student in Marburg, and they both took part in the Tambach conference in 1919. Their correspondence dating from Bultmann's review of the second edition of *Romans* in 1922 has been gathered together in a volume (V/1) of the *Gesamtausgabe*, and is translated in B. Jaspert and G.W. Bromiley (eds), *Karl Barth - Rudolf Bultmann, Letters 1922-1966* (Edinburgh, T. and T. Clark, 1982). The review was republished in J. Moltmann (ed), *Anfänge der dialektischen Theologie* (München, Kaiser Verlag, 1966) pp. 119-142. H.-Martin Rumscheidt gives an account of the correspondence in *Karl Barth in Re-view*, pp. 65-82.

12. *The Word of God and The Word of Man*, p. 24.

13. The eschatological element in his thought at this time Barth owes chiefly to the influence of Johann Christoph Blumhardt (1805-1880) and his son C.F. Blumhardt (1842-1919). For an account see Busch, pp. 83-86, and esp. H.-Martin Rumscheidt, *Revelation and Theology, An Analysis of the Barth-Harnack Correspondence of 1923* (Cambridge, CUP, 1972), pp. 7-14. Barth also welcomed the radical use which Franz Overbeck (professor of Church History at Basel, 1870-97) had made of the "radical contradiction" between "original Christian eschatology" and "the contemporary hope for the future". See his essay on Overbeck, "Unsettled Questions for Theology Today" (1920), in Karl Barth, *Theology and Church*, pp. 55-73.

14. "The Christian's Place in Society", *The Word of God and the Word of Man*, pp. 283 and 289.

15. ibid, pp. 293-4.

16. Barth's first engagement with the thought of Anselm was in relation to the soteriological work, *Why did God become a human person?* (*Cur Deus Homo?*), in 1926. The discussion of the phrase, *credo ut intellegam* (I believe in order that I may understand) began in relation to his use of Anselm in the *Christliche Dogmatik* of 1927, as Ingolf Dalferth makes clear in his foreword to the new edition of the 1931 work *Fides Quaerens Intellectum*, (eds) E. Jüngel and I.U. Dalferth, *Karl Barth Gesamtausgabe* II/1 (Zurich, TVZ, 1981), pp. VIIff. Barth responded to the discussion in the first volume of the *Church Dogmatics*, *CD* I/1 (1932, ET G.W. Bromiley, Edinburgh, T. and T. Clark, 1975), pp. 230-32.

17. "The Word of God and the Task of the Ministry", in *The Word of God and the Word of Man*, esp. pp. 206-212.

18. *Theology and Church*, p. 228.

19. ibid. pp. 230ff.

20. See Busch, p. 169.

21. See Busch, p. 133f. The warmth of Barth's regard for Peterson is evident in a letter to Martin Rade of 11 Sept. 1922, where he speaks of him as a "scholar of extraordinary fine intelligence", *Karl Barth -Martin Rade, Ein Briefwechsel*, pp. 177f.

22. Busch, pp. 168-9.

23. Busch, pp. 182-3.

24. esp. Gottlieb Söhngen in "Analogia fidei I: Gottähnlichkeit allein aus Glauben" and "Analogia fidei II: Die Einheit der Glaubenswissenschaft", in *Catholica* 3 (1934), pp. 113-136 and 176-208.

25. *Church Dogmatics* II/1, pp. 81-3

26. *Church Dogmatics* II/1, pp. 187 and 310.

27. Hans Urs von Balthasar, *Karl Barth: Darstellung und Deutung seiner Theologie* (Einsiedeln: Johannes Verlag, 1951). There is a partial ET *The Theology of Karl Barth* (New York, Holt Rinehart and Winston, 1971).

28. See esp. the 1962 essay of Eberhard Jüngel, "Die Möglichkeit theologischer Anthropologie auf dem Grunde der Analogie. Eine Untersuchung zum Analogie Verständis Karl Barths", in his *Barth-Studien*, Ökumenische Theologie: Bd. 9 (Zürich/Gütersloh, Benziger Verlag and Gerd Mohn, 1982), pp. 210-232, and H. Chavannes, *L'analogie entre Dieu et le monde selon Saint Thomas d'Aquin et selon Karl Barth* (Paris, 1969).

29. On Barth's impact on Roman Catholic theology see Emilien Lamirande, "The Impact of Karl Barth on the Catholic Church in the Last Half Century", in Martin Rumscheidt (ed), *Footnotes to a Theology* (Canadian Corporation for Studies in Religion, 1974), pp. 112-141.

30. Busch, p. 140.

31. *Revolutionary Theology*, p. 206.

32. *Karl Barth - Rudolf Bultmann*, pp. 38-9 (letter, dated 8 June, 1928).

33. ibid. p. 39.

34. *ibid.* (letter, dated 12 June, 1928), pp. 40-42. The acknowledgement of dilettantism in relation to philosophy was also made by Friedrich Schleiermacher in his well-known second letter to Lücke (1829. ET, *On the Glaubenslehre, Two Letters to Dr Lücke* (Chico, CA, Scholars Press, 1981), p. 87. The comparison is instructive.

35. *The Word of God and the Word of Man*, p. 207.

36. *ibid*. p. 206.

37. Karl Barth, *How I Changed my Mind* (Richmond, Va, John Knox Press, 1966), p. 43.

38. Quoted from *Zwischen den Zeiten*, 10 (1932), pp. 113f, in *Church Dogmatics* I/1, p. 37.

39. Tübingen, J.C.B. Mohr, 1932. Barth described this 690pp. work as "extremely loquacious", Busch, p. 219 (ET. *The Divine Imperative*, London, Lutterworth, 1937).

40. *Zwischen den Zeiten*, 10 (1932), vol. 6.

41. *The Divine Imperative*, pp. 615ff.

42. Busch, p. 224.

43. From *Nature and Grace*, A contribution to the Discussion with Karl Barth, in E. Brunner and K. Barth, *Natural Theology* (London, 1946), pp. 32-3.

44. *ibid*. p. 67.

45. Letter to Max Schoch, author of *Karl Barth Theologie in Aktion* (Frauenfeld/Stuttgart, 1967), printed in *Karl Barth, Letters 1961-1968* (Edinburgh, T. and T. Clark, 1981), p. 270.

46. "Intellectual Autobiography" in C.W. Kegley (ed), *The Theology of Emil Brunner* (New York, Macmillan, 1962), p. 10.

47. *Letters 1961-1968*, pp. 270 and 337; compare Busch, p. 189.

49. J.C. McLelland, "Philosophy and Theology - A Family Affair (Karl and Heinrich Barth)", M. Rumscheidt, *Footnotes to a Theology*, pp. 30-52.

50. See above, footnote 2.

51. On this aspect of Barth, see the fine review of Busch's biography by Hans Frei in *Karl Barth in Re-View*, pp. 95-116, esp. pp.100f.

52 *CD* I/2, p. 729.

53. *CD* I/2, p. 732.

54. *CD* I/2, p. 859.

55. Compare esp. the response of the distinguished and influential British philosopher of religion, D.M. MacKinnon in his essay "Philosophy and Christology", contributed to *Essays in Christology in honour of Karl Barth* (1956), and his Cambridge inaugural lecture "Borderlands of Theology" (1961), both reprinted in *Borderlands of Theology* (London, Lutterworth, 1968). See also P.G. Wignall, "D.M. MacKinnon: An Introduction to his Early Theological Writings" in S.W. Sykes and D.J. Holmes, *New Studies in Theology* (London, Duckworth, 1980), pp. 65-94.

KARL BARTH
Fate and Idea in Theology

*Lectures delivered at the Hochschulinstitut
in Dortmund, February-March, 1929.
Translation of "Schicksal und Idée" in Theologische
Fragen und Antworten*

The title announced for these lectures may have provoked astonishment. Let me briefly explain the title, and this will lead us directly into the subject matter.

"Fate and Idea" — what does that mean? When I was invited to give these lectures and had to announce my topic, I picked this particular pair of concepts almost accidentally from a whole series of others which could also have expressed what I meant. I might just as well have said: "reality and truth," or "nature and spirit," or "the objective and the non-objective," or "the conditioned and the unconditioned," or "being and thinking," or "heteronomy and autonomy," or "experience and reason." I might also have said: "realism and nominalism," or "romanticism and idealism."

You can see that the basic problem of all philosophy is at stake, one which can be expressed in various ways. Whenever it probes more or less deeply into human existence, philosophy eventually strikes upon what these and similar concepts indicate, namely, the two boundaries of human thought. It strikes, in other words, upon the problem of how these two boundaries are related to one another, upon the question of their priority (because one might take precedence over the other), and upon the problem of their higher unity. We will use the terms "fate and idea," because they are especially close to the life experience from which the problem of these boundaries, apparently so theoretical, arises.

To designate these boundaries as "fate and idea" is to imply that not only our act of thinking but also our act of living (which also involves thinking) is determined in a two-fold way. We thereby point to these boundaries as weighty subjects, as powers that bear upon us, as matters with which we very much have "to do." We live our fate or destiny, yet we also live our project or idea. The other conceptual pairs describe this more theoretically. When we say "fate and idea," we will not want to forget the theoretical horizons toward which they direct us, sometimes more narrowly, sometimes more broadly. However, when it comes to discussing the meaning of this situation for theology, we will be glad our particular terms reminded us that we are not dealing here with empty concepts. If we were we would not be dealing with genuine concepts; genuine concepts are never empty concepts. Rather, we may say for the time being that what concerns us here are existential forces.

"Fate and Idea *in Theology*" — that is to be the topic. The focus is not to be historical, but fundamental and systematic. An account of the history of the problem in theology itself, or of its theological status today, would be a major undertaking and cannot be attempted here. By "theology" we understand that discipline of the church — in fact the Christian, Protestant church — oriented toward God as the object of its proclamation. Theology is thus related to the church as its theological sphere of life, just as medicine is related to the physiological, philosophy to the psychological (in the broadest sense), and jurisprudence to the sociological sphere of life. Theology is an academic discipline (*Wissenschaft*). That is, it is a technically ordered investigation into the truth about God as the object of ecclesiastical proclamation. It thus does not investigate and teach the truth about God as such. For theology as for all other academic disciplines, God as such is a hypothesis, a limit-concept, which cannot come into consideration as an object of human inquiry and knowledge. Theology, rather, investigates and teaches the truth about God as he is proclaimed and should be proclaimed in the church.

Proclaimed in that way, God becomes the content of the church's particular sphere of life. Theology relates to this sphere as a technical discipline, it finds the possibility of its earthly location within it, and upon this ground human beings can be theologians. That is how God becomes the object of theology. And that is why we confessed ourselves just a short while ago so explicitly to the theology of the Christian, Protestant church. What theology deals with is the God who is proclaimed to us. We can ask whether that really occurs for us and whether we are thereby called to take part in theological work. Should we regard ourselves as called to this communal task, then we are affirming that God is proclaimed to us. With our stance in the church as the setting where this takes place, we are affirming that no other possibility exists for us than Christian, Protestant theology. If at the same time we wanted to engage in, say, Buddhist or Catholic theology, we would be denying what we have just affirmed. In the empty space above the churches and the confessions, there is no theology. At best what would exist there would be the problem of God as such, a God to be sought for in a *progressus in infinitum*. That is a problem, however, for which there is no technical discipline. Theology is possible only as a theology of the proclaimed God — the God whom we do not first have to seek but who has given and still gives himself to be found by us, the God who has revealed and still reveals himself, the God who sends forth his Word.

Theology can know about God only to the extent that God makes himself accessible to us, but to that extent theology really does claim to know about God. The church's proclamation is grounded in God's Word and lives in service to that Word — God's Word as it is said to her, the Christian, Protestant church. What theology then investigates and teaches has to do with what may be contained in God's Word as the truth proclaimed in this situation. Theology thus has God as its object, but only to the extent that, as Thomas Aquinas once profoundly remarked,[1] theology has God as its subject, even if that subject is most highly hidden. That is, theology has God as its object only to the extent that it strives to have absolutely no other origin than the communication which God actually gives of himself. No step, not even the smallest, can be dared by theology except on the ground that God allows himself to be found before we have ever sought him. For indeed the church, too, dares to venture its proclamation only on the basis of this authentic communication, only in obedience, only in the consciousness that the church is not ultimately the subject of what it proclaims, but stands completely in the service of this communication.

But just as the church is very much a human sphere of life and its proclamation very much a human venture, so is theology very much the human undertaking of a technical or academic discipline. Its tools are nothing more than ordinary human thought and speech with their own definite laws, possibilities and limitations. In each of its respective stages of development, theology works with the same human thought as any other technical discipline. Just as the church finds itself in the framework of the state but does not exist in competition with it (although the church understands itself as a community, indeed, as *the* community), so theology understands itself as (the) fundamental reflection about human existence as discussed within the framework of philosophy.[2]

Theology claims to say more than philosophy can say. It claims to offer and to be human knowledge that rests upon a recognition of divine revelation. Yet theology can in no way make the truth of its claim directly visible, to say nothing of making it verifiable, simply because theology can never be and offer itself as anything other than human knowledge. Despite the divine origin and object of its knowledge, theology has no divinely unambiguous categories at its disposal, none which might not be countered or cancelled by categories from elsewhere. It has no categories by which it might conclusively be able to differentiate its knowledge, the knowledge of God's Word, from the knowledge of the philosophers. It can never say the specific thing which it has to say as theology such that the philosopher could not also say it in a pinch, perhaps meaning something completely different. For that is precisely what theology will never be able to prove to the philosopher with final triumphant clarity — that the philosopher really means something different.

Among the philosophers things will always go for the theologian as they did for Aaron when he cast down his rod before Pharaoh and it became a serpent. "Then Pharaoh summoned the wise men and the sorcerers; and they also, the magicians of Egypt, did the same by their secret arts. For every man cast down his rod, and they became serpents" (Ex. 7:11-12). Within human limits the theologian can certainly come up with signs that are definite and relatively extraordinary. These signs might well receive some amazed or even embarrassing notice. Why was it that theology frequently used to call itself *philosophia sacra* or *christiana*? Was it humility? Was it self-consciousness? By producing these relatively extraordinary signs — I mean by developing a Christian dogmatics, a conceptual scheme grounded in the Bible — the theologian is supposed to serve the truth of God's Word by bringing it to validity as a technical discipline.

Good for him if that is what he does, if he really does that and not something else. Good for him if in the framework of philosophy he is nothing but a human thinker, a *philosophus* among others, reflecting fundamentally on the conception of human existence, and yet is still a witness to thinking based on divine revelation. Good for him if in the shroud of the completely similar,which he too can think and say by himself, he speaks of the completely dissimilar; if in the shroud of what is merely relatively extraordinary, in which he has a right to speak, that absolutely extraordinary reality becomes manifest which only God can speak; if while speaking in the world yet not of this world, he nonetheless even in the full humanity of his words really speaks of God. Then he is not only called a theologian, then he is a theologian. Then he says what only the theologian can say, what even the philosopher could not say as a philosopher but only as a theologian. Then the other thing is fulfilled which also stands written in the passage: "But Aaron's rod swallowed up their rods" (Ex. 7:12). "I cannot teach, preach, write, pray, or give thanks except by these physical instruments, which are required for the performance of these activities. Nevertheless, these activities do not come from the flesh and do not originate there; they are given and revealed divinely from heaven."[3]

But it is the miracle of God if that happens — not the nature or art of the theologian, but simply grace. Grace is imponderable, one cannot take it for oneself, it can only be received. If we want to disregard this great limit to the theologian's activity, or the great fulfillment which alone can make it meaningful, then it needs to be said that considered by itself this undertaking is completely exposed and dangerous. Only one thing keeps it from being doomed to failure: the presupposition of divine miracle. For it turns out that Aaron with his clever trick cannot avoid taking his place in a brotherly way beside the Egyptian magicians. It turns out that of himself he can do no more than they can do. It happens that even *philosophia sacra* is in any case *philosophia*, that at best *theologia* can come into being only under the presupposition of God's gracious miracle.

The great temptation and danger consists in this, that the theologian will actually become what he seems to be — a philosopher. Without having heard what is said to us about reality by the Lord of reality, or without having heeded what he has heard, the theologian might dare to say the necessary thing to himself and to others. He might dare to say it not on the basis of the fact that it is said to him, but in the confidence that he is basically in a position to say it of his own accord.

The situation of the theologian over against the philosopher is something like this: Let us grant for the sake of argument that he, the theologian, might have said something with his relatively extraordinary sign which carries the force of divine grace. Suppose also that it would be intelligible to the philosopher either wholly or partly as truth. What then? Will the philosopher respect it in the sense that it was meant — as something said in recognition of the divine Word? Will he thus let himself be called to listen to this Word? Perhaps he will. But who or what can force him to do that? Who or what can prevent him from taking it as a welcome and deep enrichment of what he knows already about human reality? (For after all it was uttered only in the form of human knowledge.) What is to prevent him from *also* saying it as much as ever (with no intention of serving God's Word) in the conviction that this too is something one can simply say to oneself — probably with the proviso that the cumbersome symbolic language of theology needs to be done away with or quietly reinterpreted?

Won't this process, which has happened a thousand times — all philosophy has in fact had its origin in some kind of theology — force the theologian to consider whether he might not do better to look more favorably upon the human capacity for saying the necessary thing to oneself? Especially when he now confronts the fact that the philosopher can say everything which he, the theologian, can say? For by having to heed God's Word he has to speak in such a crabbed, constricted and paradoxical way. The philosopher, on the other hand, is in a position to say it all so much better, more freely, more universally, so fully in the name of every human being!

Why shouldn't theology, under the force of this claim, simply and honorably become philosophy? Isn't that what it already is? How will it prove that it isn't? Is the best that theology can say really any different from the deepest thing philosophy can say, only better, more accessibly, and more comprehensively, in the name of every human being? How will theology show that things are otherwise, that its most distinctive content is not something which can also be said philosophically? How will theology show that things are otherwise when as already noted it cannot leave the context of philosophy by its own powers, when theology can only raise its particular signs within that context, yet without being able to validate them of itself as signs that are really distinctive? How could it be otherwise?

At no time is theology ever *not* in danger, ever *not* in temptation. Theology stands under the insufferable pressure of a situation where it can speak only humanly and where this occurs so much better in philosophy. Indeed philosophy manages to speak profoundly in human language without hearing the Word, without the troublesome connection to Bible and church, and without the recurrent counter-question that constantly casts doubt upon the idea of a divine miracle confirming a human word. Just as theology is tempted by philosophy, so too the church stands in the parallel danger and temptation of either trying to become the state or of being absorbed into the state.

This ever possible betrayal of theology to philosophy can occur openly and consciously. There have been times when theologians frankly felt compelled to be not only in the world, where they were anyway, but also really and recognizably of the world. They were like those North African Christians who, according to Cyprian's report, during a time of persecution showed up in such droves to make the commanded sacrifice of incense to the gods that the presiding praetor was at a loss for what to do and finally ended up by granting clemency to the whole poor gang of apostates.

More often, however, it is a matter of *penetration pacifique* from the philosophical side. The theologians let themselves be consciously impressed and are then caught unawares; theology in this case would never consider abdicating overtly. Rather, it holds its own in the midst of the great din, perhaps even claiming to be positive, orthodox theology. It continues to affirm its intention of having nothing but God's Word as the origin and object of its strivings. It continues to hold Christ, the Bible and perhaps even dogma in high esteem. The church continues to suppose that it retains a theology which will function as a technical discipline about the proclaimed God and which will nurture a rising generation of preachers. The church is perhaps even rather pleased that theology seems to be right at home in the academic world — a hopeful sign for the church's own possibility of success in the perhaps even more difficult world of affairs. For in covertly becoming philosophy, theology needs only to accept a few small shifts in accent, undertake a few minor adjustments, adopt a few of the harmless reinterpretations or deletions which philosophy suggests might be useful to dogmatics.

However, if the abyss separating a theology that really is theology from one which is actually philosophy turns out to be only the breadth of a crack, it is nevertheless an abyss. The danger and temptation which constantly surrounds the theologian might make conscious betrayal seem humanly and objectively attractive. Might it not seem improper for Aaron — who after all really couldn't to any more than Pharaoh's magicians — to remain Aaron rather than finally becoming an Egyptian magician himself? This temptation and danger is plainly a great cause for concern. And theology's defense, or let us say more cautiously, its watchfulness, against that temptation and danger constitutes the great aspiration of a theology which keenly sizes up its task. For in that case theology will appreciate how unprotected its work really is, how much all guarantees must be renounced in pursuing it, how much it must simply be ventured in obedience. Thinking and speaking humanly, all too humanly, yet nevertheless letting God's Word be said — that is the task of theology. It is the task of a theology which, granted God's grace, thinks and speaks not about those boundaries of human thought, but with all possible objectivity about God.

This brings us directly to our theme. Theology is a technical discipline concerned about God, about the God proclaimed by his church. It is, however, a human discipline. It involves a fundamental reflection upon reality by means of that very same thought which is also the tool of the philosophers. Therefore, it cannot fail that those two boundaries of human existence, the basic problem of all philosophy, will also arise in theology and play a decisive role. Even in theology we will not be able to get around this two-fold aspect of reality. Because our inquiry proceeds by human thought, it meets us of its own accord.

At this point the critical question is decided as to whether we are doing theology or only philosophy. Here is where the temptation or danger is or is not resisted. Here we do or do not get stuck on that two-fold aspect of reality which shows up in thinking not governed by the Word of God. To put it concretely, here is where we face the temptation of seeking and finding God in fate or God in idea. On the strength of the fact that our thinking is governed by God's Word, we are tempted to surpass the relativity of this two-fold aspect — not through a conceptual synthesis of our own, but by attributing this aspect to God himself as the Lord of all reality.

Theology's critical reflection not only on its nearness to philosophy — a nearness as necessary as it is perilous — but also on the nearness of God's Word to the last and deepest of human words — that is the topic of these lectures. According to their introductory nature, I think of them as clarifying not only the danger and temptation of theology, but also the watchfulness incumbent upon it.

I

We will begin by discussing the theological character of the concept of fate. The first naive steps in human reflection on humanity's relation to God doubtless lead in this direction. The relationship between fate and idea is not symmetrical. We do not stand as it were at the midpoint between the two. On the contrary, it will always seem more natural for us to seek God in our fate or in fate our God. Knowledge is first and foremost a knowledge of experience or of existing reality. When it proceeds to clarify itself critically, by advancing into knowledge of truth, then that is simply a second step which presupposes the first.

At this point it can be confirmed that theological knowledge does not occur in its own special framework, but in the same one occupied by philosophical knowledge. For we are obviously advancing here toward the objective, the given, and the actual. "God is" — what does that mean if not that God takes part in being? Then of course the next proposition leads to the idea that God is himself being, the origin and perfection of everything that is. In their classical form, as set forth by Thomas Aquinas, these propositions combine with a third which can logically be regarded as the consequence, namely, everything that is as such participates in God. Everything that is exists as mere creature in greatest dissimilarity to the Creator, yet by having being it exists in greatest similarity to the Creator. That is what is meant by *analogia entis*.

The realist confidently supposes that in what is given he is able to encounter something similar to God, and this confidence gives definition to his teaching. For he teaches that God must be inferred from the given (necessarily from the given and not from anywhere else). (What we have here is a kind of basic orientation which does not let itself be further grounded; it is what the realist simply accepts.) God is ontologically and noetically the fate of humanity. It is thus the case that we stand in relation to God by virtue of the fact that we ourselves *are* and that things outside of us *are*. We ourselves and things outside of us — realism possesses this double aspect. What is given has both an inward and an outward dimension, a subjective and an objective facticity. *Analogia entis* means the dissimilarity and similarity to God which I myself have as knower and the thing outside me has as the known. That is what it has to mean if those two givens are to become for me something similar to God (*similitudo Dei*) and if I am supposed to know God from them.

Classical theism like that of Aquinas's stresses both aspects equally. It will balance the scales as skillfully as possible between outer and inner experience, between God's objective and subjective givenness. Within the bounds of realism, however, the possibility exists that one side might be weighted more heavily than the other or perhaps even placed in conflict with the other. After a time one will then have to return to some form of the neglected counterpart. Experiential theology of all sorts swings back and forth, now representing God's givenness as inward and subjective, now as outward and objective.

A few examples can easily make it clear that these conflicts are not irresolvable, that they beckon to one another, that in one way or another they finally instantiate the same general conception. Was anything really new said to Wallenstein, who while gazing into the stars heard a voice tell him, "In your heart are the stars of your fate." Or is it anything new if psychoanalysis, one of the "unacknowledged religions" of our day, should take its place alongside astrology? This circle apparently has to be closed again and again. As a circle it is all'too true and genuine. Wasn't Luther on target when he lumped together the Anabaptist claim that the Holy Spirit was given in the individual's heart, with the Roman Catholic claim that it was given in papal authority, rejecting them both as religious enthusiasm? Or don't those two feuding siblings, pietism and rationalism, actually belong together, since the one elevates the subjective religious experience of the inner world into the criterion of theology, while the other does the same thing with the objective experience of the outer world?

Was it really a split and contradiction in Schleiermacher's theology when in his youth he wanted to give the name God to the universe as piously experienced, whereas in maturity he sought God in the feeling of absolute dependence as such? Does not the peculiar construction of his christology (to say nothing of the whole development of modern theology, vexed by Feuerbach at the one end and D. F. Strauss at the other) point to the fact that a psychologistic empiricism will eventually call forth one that is historicist, just as the latter if neglected will call forth the former? Faith and history, history and faith — how often have we heard this little stanza since those days? What does Wobbermin's psychology of religion teach us with its "circle" if not that here both sides are to be dealt with — Thomas Aquinas's worthy equilibrium will soon be achieved yet again — in the same manner as givens? Or is Martin Kaehler's science of Christian doctrine any less realistic when its pendulum swings to Christ on one side and faith on the other? Didn't the "positive" theology which commenced with unprecedented subjectivism in Hoffmann and Frank, find forceful completion in Erich Schäder's "theocentric" theology — and then through the mouth of this same Schäder find itself forced to proclaim that the God of Christian theology cannot be any other than "the God of our consciousness"?

It really isn't much more than a domestic quarrel resting on a kind of optical illusion if the objectivists and the subjectivists, the theologians of experience and the theologians of history, the anthropocentrists and the theocentrists occasionally talk past each other. They ought to understand each other all the same, not taking their in-house "tensions" too tragically, but recognizing in Thomas Aquinas the peace that is higher than their reasoning (*Vernunft*). We are obviously dealing here with the sort of theological empiricism that discovers God in *fate* — a fate that befalls human beings inwardly-outwardly, subjectively-objectively, something which becomes all too powerful for them and takes them prisoner, setting them in absolute dependence.

What should we say to that? Certainly we must say that theological realism in all its varieties articulates a genuine and serious theological problem. Theology cannot answer the questions, where is God? and who or what is God?, without starting down this path. If we are going to talk about God as the *object* of theology, then we will already be advancing a typically realist proposition. How could we get away from God's objectivity completely, even if we ardently wanted to place it in quotation marks? Is theology perhaps to present itself as a discipline without an object of inquiry? Wouldn't it be pitiful if theology wanted to retreat to the notion that its object was not God but merely faith — as if it would not immediately fall into the same dilemma about how to deal with God as the object of faith or whether perhaps faith too was something without an object? At the very least we cannot get around ascribing the quality of being to God, being under quite definite conditions, but certainly being. The proposition that "God is" is a realist utterance not easily dispensed with if theology is not to fall into mystical silence the first time it ventures to speak. And the situation does not get any easier but even more exacting when we recall that by the term God we do not mean some sort of "God as such," but rather, according to our agreement about the nature of theology, the God of the Christian church, the God revealed in his Word.

How can we speak of revelation without speaking of God's givenness? "The Word became flesh and dwelt among us" — what does that mean if not that the Word, and hence the God with whom we have to do, entered into our own particular mode of being, that of nature and history? Jesus Christ as the Word of God to us and therefore himself as God is the content of revelation. And also the Holy Spirit, who illumines the Word for us and us for the Word, is himself God, is the content of revelation. Nor can we neglect here the original, foundational and central datum of Christian ethics — the simple givenness of the Thou for the I. "My neighbor" — according to Matt. 25 is not that the great *similitudo Dei*? Once we have said Christ and the Holy Spirit, and therefore Thou and I, have we not articulated the two poles of theological realism: the outer and the inner, the objective and the subjective? Does not God's being revealed mean at least this much as well, that God becomes an object of our experience? What is revelation — God's revelation — if not God's making himself accessible to our experience, if not God's giving over of himself to that objective-subjective *similitudo* of himself, if not God's letting himself be found within and without, his givenness there for *us here* and for us here *there*? What does revelation mean if not that God is our fate?

Simply to recall the concept of revelation ought to bring home to us that in realism we can detect one of the legitimate and indispensable aspirations of all genuine theology, namely, the concern to understand God as an actuality. The exact foreign word corresponding to the German *Wirklichkeit* here would not be "reality," but "actuality" (just as it is certain that here facticity and objectivity are within hailing distance). Our life is a process of perceiving ourselves, our world, and the two in indissoluble correlation. It runs its course as an experience of actuality, as a series of operations that happen to us and with us. That is what allows us to connect the concept of reality with that of fate. At least at first we judge the things, that is, the possibilities that we meet, according to the standard of reality, or by whether and to what extent they are fateful to us. Do I experience them? Do I experience them in the unity and totality of inner and outer experience? Are they *real* for me? Are they real for *me*? How do they concern me? Whatever does not concern me wholly and finally, how can that be anything for me but a nothing? Act means being, and being can only mean act.

It should not be surprising that instinctively we even measure God by this standard, at least as a first step in our reflecting about God. How could God be anything other than real, real at least in the same sense that I experience myself and the world in which I live — real as act, being and fate? Don't we have to pose this question simply by virtue of the concept of revelation? Indeed, if we are here presupposing revelation, won't we immediately have to add, how could God be anything other than real in the preeminent sense? For by this presupposition aren't we compelled to think of a God who is neither a second reality alongside ourselves and our world, nor merely another name for the reality of self and world? God therefore is the reality through which and in which the reality of self and world is real. As the preeminent reality God is *causa prima, ens realissimum* and *actus purus*, the reality of all reality. Yet precisely as such, *in similitudine*, God is an object of our experience, experience always understood in the two-fold sense of outer and inner.

The thought of God thereby shows itself to be serious. To be taken seriously this thought must express our fate. It must be an expression of reality, indeed of the great reality which includes and surpasses all other reality in itself. It must represent the one reality present in all other reality, hidden but not entirely hidden there. It acquires legitimacy as a thought about experience.

How should theology, which does its work in the same framework as philosophy, the framework of human thinking, expect to be true in any other way? How else should theology expect to do justice to the needs of life if not as realist theology? How in particular should it expect to do justice to itself as a theology of the Christian church, to the need for a Christian proclamation guided by human thinking, if not by this kind of realism? Whether one will finally prefer a theology of absolute dependence or a theology of faith and history, a theology of Roman Catholic authority or a theology of religious immediacy, is a matter that may be safely left to a discussion and moderate use of Wobbermin's religious-psychological circle. And once more, can't all these theologies, though diverse among themselves, appeal to the sheer facticity of revelation, above all to revelation as christianly understood? Shouldn't "realist" be synonymous with "Christian" to the extent that Christ and the Holy Spirit doubtlessly signify for us the reality of God in the world?

As these reflections have already made clear, a critical analysis of this position cannot mean a twilight of the gods. The aspirations of theological realism are too genuine and necessary for anyone to suppose that a simple and sweeping rejection would not mean tossing out the baby with the bath water. No theology can afford not to share completely the intentions evident here. Anyone who wanted to reject this position *in globo* would not be a particularly good theologian, not even a particularly good Protestant theologian. Instead he would merely show himself to be an idealist, and not a particularly sophisticated one at that. In any case such a person would not be suited to deal with the problem of theology. A theology not open to the aspirations of realism would be neither Protestant nor Christian. For it would be neither Protestant nor Christian not to want to articulate the full meaning intended by the idea of "God in fate."

At this point we must again remind ourselves that theology cannot be theology unless it thinks and speaks of God on the basis of God's Word. Theology must thus remain on guard lest it end up thinking and saying something entirely different than what is required of it by God's Word. As theology unavoidably entrusts itself to the guidance of realist thought (that is, to a particular form of human *logos*), such vigilance cannot be dropped — regardless of how much this guide may appeal in a secondary way to revelation! It is by no means obvious that the guidance realism offers can simply be equated with the final and authentic guidance to be received from God's Word. Nor is it obvious that the two will never disagree. There can be no doubt, however, that guidance from God's Word takes place in the same general framework where that other (human) guide offers services that cannot simply be rejected. Theology must therefore pose a certain question to itself and to realism. The answer will determine not whether, but to what extent, theology may think and speak realistically.

The heart of the matter goes back to what we have called realism's basic orientation — its simple confidence that via certain precise conceptual formulations God can be found in a subjective-objective givenness, and that therefore the *similitudo Dei* must also occur in knower and known. Do we stand before God — the God, let me stress, or revelation — in such a position that realism's basic orientation could and may be adopted wholesale as the basic orientation for theology? Is such naive confidence really grounded in God's revelation? Does revelation really do no more than confirm and reinforce supernaturally a naively presupposed human capacity and necessity apparently somehow given with our existence as such?

That is in fact how Thomas Aquinas presented the matter. For him the experience of God is a unique possibility at the disposal of human existence, precisely by virtue of revelation, because even at its lowest level human existence participates in the *lumen divinum* of the highest level. *Gratia non destruit, sed supponit et perficit naturam*. (Grace does not destroy, but supplements and perfects nature.) *Analogia entis* means that every existing being and we as human beings participate in the *similitudo Dei*. The experience of God becomes an inherent human possibility and necessity. The Protestant realists did not adopt this construct, which Thomas developed in an extraordinarily penetrating and consistent manner; or if they did adopt it, they did so only in fragments. But with regard to the possibility of experiencing God, is their confidence therefore any the less — confidence that Christians as human beings are quite capable of such an experience?

If the basic orientation of realism is not to be something completely different from that of the person who hears God's Word, then the presupposition of an inherent human capacity will have to be met with skepticism and astonishment, if not outright rejection. God's Word does not confirm and reinforce the naive confidence that it is possible for human beings to experience God. On the contrary, by mediating such an experience, it shakes that confidence rather severely. Otherwise how would it be God's Word? In contrast to the whole range of possible human experience, the Word says something new — not something more strongly and clearly that human beings knew anyway and that they could also experience in some other way.

That is in fact how things always stand between human beings and God's Word. God's Word announces something new to them. It comes to them as light into the darkness. It always comes to them as sinners, as forgiving and thus as judging grace. In relation to it human beings are never once those who are already pardoned, and thus those to whom God's Word no longer or only partially proclaims something new. If they hear something that basically they already know, then they certainly hear something other than God's Word. "God resists the proud but gives grace to the humble." Human beings are always pardoned in this way, that God's grace comes to them, not otherwise, not beforehand and also not afterwards. The heavenly manna in the wilderness does not, as we know, let itself be saved up. "What have you that you did not receive?"

Therefore, that possibility and necessity, that capacity for experiencing God, cannot be understood as something "natural." It cannot be understood as something given with human existence as such, nor as something subsequently connected with human existence. Not even by an appeal to a *gratia inhaerens* can it be understood in this way. No inherent grace or capacity for grace can be claimed by virtue of which the knower and the known would exist in relation to God through the *ana-*

logia entis. That is the first and basic question that we have to direct to theological realists of whatever stripe. With their thesis about the possibility of experiencing God, have they really taken into account that it is grace which encounters sinners?

Because what encounters sinners is grace, God's givenness to us and to the world — God's givenness in his revelation — cannot be understood as though it were somehow accessible to a set of precise conceptual formulations as such. It cannot be understood as though divine acts occur, or as though their effects appear, without an actor. It cannot be understood as though God's reality were accessible apart from God himself as the performer of his work — which is the Word that comes to us. God is therefore given to us neither in the givenness of history and nature nor in that of our own consciousness. In these abstractions from the event of grace, God is not given to us. For grace is the event in which God comes to us in his Word, an event over which God has sole control, and which is strictly momentary. Otherwise God could not be distinguished from a hidden feature of reality as such. He could not be distinguished from fate. The possibility of experiencing God cannot be understood as something given by fate. God distinguishes himself from fate by the fact that he is not so much there as rather that he comes.

Confidence in God's self-giving is therefore rather different from realism's confidence in God's givenness. The former involves no underside of horror and dread before the non-givenness of this God. It involves no dread before the fact that our own reality and that of the world, and even that in which the Bible and church are given to us, can always be anything but *similitudo Dei*. It involves no dread before the fact that God not only reveals but also hides himself in his revelation, because it is a revealing and not a state of being revealed. Therefore, in a theology of God's Word we can think and speak realistically only with these reservations. We can think and speak realistically only by presupposing the act-character of God's reality. Although Thomas himself laid great weight on this matter, it is being propounded here in a completely different way than was true in his case. We can think and speak realistically only by presupposing that the very thing realism posits — the possibility and necessity of finding God in experience — is such that it must be taken up, negated and transformed (*aufgehoben*). Such a possibility and necessity, in other words, is a matter of God's free will, not our will. Not even subsequently and *per infusionem* does it become a function of our will. The reason is not merely because we have a weak, creaturely will made even weaker through sin. It is rather because our will is perverse, fundamentally incapable of knowing God and of acting obediently toward him. That is why the *similitudo Dei* has to be given to us in every moment as something divinely new.

This basic question leads to further questions about details. One might ask, for example, about the possibility of an inward experience of God. We must beware of calling that into question. The Holy Spirit would certainly be denied if we wanted to dispute the possibility of his witness in our hearts, of really seeking and finding God within us. When it comes to the realists of inward experience, however, we will have to ask whether they really mean the Holy Spirit with their talk of God within. We have to ask whether they have considered that the Holy Spirit is no less God than the Father and the Son, and thus whether they are prepared to preserve the distance appropriate even toward the God who can be experienced inwardly. But in that case God will be sought in the Word spoken to us, not in the experience produced by that Word. The peace of God will then above all be distinguished from any peace we might make with ourselves instead of being confused with it. There will then be no question of understanding God from ourselves, but only of understanding ourselves from God. Nor will there be any question of elevating our hearts into God's throne. We are only inquiring. Yet we have to ask the theological realists in all seriousness whether they realize that the supposed inward experience of God is given to none but pardoned felons. We have to ask whether they realize that the examination has to be the most severe precisely when it comes to the possibilities of Christian experience. We have to ask, in short, whether we are really doing theology or merely realistic philosophy. The latter is done so vacantly by many they know not what they do.

When it comes to the counterpart, the side concerned about outward experience, the question must be posed somewhat differently. Once again, Christ would certainly be denied if we wanted to place this possibility in doubt. When realists claim to have God as the object of experience, however, we have to ask whether it is really Christ who is meant, whether Christ's deity is really taken seriously. It sounds suspicious when, as often happens, history with great fanfare is said to be a neutral concept. And it sounds more than suspicious when Christ is placed in a series with other great historical figures, and the attempt is seriously made by means of comparison to demonstrate that he is God's revealer. The suspicions arise for at least two reasons. Not only is an untenable concept of history being presupposed, as though there were a history in general within which God's revelation were available like water in a glass. An untenable concept of human nature is also being presupposed, as though human beings themselves possessed the capacity for ascertaining what is or is not revelation, as though they had at their disposal a criterion by which they might recognize and acknowledge Christ. If that is the bottom line, then one can only observe that what is taking place is not theology so much as philosophy in a realist vein. If in the case of inward experience we had to ask about keeping the proper distance, then here we have to ask whether the experience of God being discussed is really so inescapable.

The hesitation necessary toward theological realism — I intentionally do not put it any stronger than that — can be summarized like this. Doesn't realism come dangerously near to conceiving of God as given by fate at the very point where God has nothing in common with fate, namely, at the point of his coming? Aren't we threatened here with the idea of a God whose being is merely there instead of a God who comes? Wouldn't it perhaps be better for this God to be called simply nature? And might it not be better for the theology of this particular God to be called demonology rather than theology? We don't have to figure out whether or to what extent this actually needs to be said about the theological realists. As a matter of fact it would be difficult to determine whether with these questions we have not departed hopelessly from a Thomas or a Schleiermacher, to say nothing of the realists in contemporary theology. But we did need to speak of the boundary that visibly emerges here, of the danger against which theology must remain on the alert. The *Deus sive natura* is not the God who reveals himself in his Word.

II

The concept of idea, to which we now turn, distinguishes thinking that has been chastened and strengthened by critical reflection. It typifies knowledge that exists, so to speak, at one remove under the sign of the question: What is truth? It thereby seeks a kind of supreme court where reality can be considered, legitimated as such, and finally supplied with foundations. It seeks for something not given, non-objective and unconditioned, namely, for the noetic and ontological presupposition of all that is given, objective and conditioned. It therefore asks about something that cannot be seen, but can only be viewed as the essential content of all that is visible — about the place where everything visible is reconstituted on a higher plane. It asks in short about idea.

Idealist thinking is critically chastened: it worries about the realist's naive confidence. It poses a fundamental question about what the realist simply takes for granted — about how self-evident the way really is from object to subject, and from subject to object. In other words, it asks about where the givenness of this correlation comes from, and about the limits to knowledge within it. Idealist thinking is also critically strengthened, however, for by posing this question it discovers something not given over against the given subject and object. It discovers itself as a criterion that must at least be taken into account. Whether openly or secretly, it discovers itself as original and superior to mere being.

So, as thinking at once chastened and strengthened, humble and proud, idealism in the person of Plato once entered the lists against all pre-socratic philosophy, opposed the medieval realists in the form of nominalism, and later took on modern empiricists of all varieties with Descartes and then with Kant and his disciples. Idealism means the self-reflection of the spirit over against nature. It discovers a correlation between thinking and truth. The creative logos becomes the source from which subject and object are given in correlation. Reason is exalted over the objective and subjective power of fate, and is used to gain mastery over the limitation fate imposes on human existence.

How could theology or thinking concerned with God not be encountered on this path? One might even ask whether philosophical idealism would ever exist without the general problem of theology. Strictly speaking, isn't it the concept of God that provides the impetus for carrying through the project of critical idealist thinking? Be that as it may, the reverse is certainly true that no theology has ever avoided the general problem of idealism.

As already hinted, even realist theology cannot be theology without drawing heavily on idealism. For doesn't realism itself go so far in analyzing the given as to talk about *analogia entis* and *similitudo Dei*?

To demonstrate a conceptually necessary presupposition, the condition for the possibility of thinking about given being, doesn't Thomas develop his proof of God's existence and his *via negativa*? Doesn't he attain his God-concept as a concept of pure being or pure act by abstracting from given being as such? Wherever the concept of God is being taken seriously, God's givenness must not only be distinguished, but fundamentally distinguished, from all other being. In relation to all other being God's being takes on the ascribed quality of non-givenness and to that extent even non-being. Even when it comes to knowledge of God illumined by grace and based on revelation, Thomas writes that it "joins us to him as to an unknown."[4] Nor can a comparable critical knowledge of God's non-givenness be denied to Schleiermacher's realism, even though it is more oriented toward and interested in subjectivity. Realism is not vulnerable to attack on this flank, for its lack of caution is limited. It isn't as if it too did not know that God's otherness and hiddenness bestows singularity on what stands over against it as the subject and object of human knowing. It isn't as if realism too did not know:

> Soul, should you want this to find,
> Seek it by nary a creature,
> Leave all that is earthly behind,
> Swing yourself up over nature.

Wherever this "swing yourself up over nature" prevails, there we will have to speak of idealist theology. For at that point the shrewd question about God's hiddenness and otherness beyond the existentially given is not posed (as it is with realism) as merely a secondary adjustment, but as something primary and basic. A tendency toward mysticism emerges by which an immediate knowledge of God is regarded not only as the top but as the very root of the tree. The kinship between idealist and mystical thinking suggests that idealist theology does not necessarily originate from or point back to a philosophical system. Just as we avoided dismissing theological realism as a disguised philosophy, so we will now have to do the same justice to theological idealism. It is possible to be a theological realist or idealist without being tainted by the corresponding philosophy. It is lamentable that in the history of theology (including the present), it has been imagined again and again that one's opponent can be dismissed simply by pointing to a realist or idealist philosopher who stands in the wings. It is beyond question that an idealist theologian can sincerely and genuinely be connected to God's revelation and to its witness in Bible and church. Should anyone be so scrupulous as to turn away this food for reasons of conscience, one might take pleasure in devouring it before his very eyes for the sake of evangelical freedom — after having duly instructed him from Paul and Luther.

Isn't the idealist principle of differentiating the non-given from the given justified by our need to understand revelation as *God's* revelation in contrast to whatever else might somehow be revealed? And isn't all theology a matter of understanding, a matter of rendering to ourselves an account of God in the form of human concepts, in other words, in the form of intellectual work, by abstracting from the given and interpreting the given? Doesn't it have to be said that all theology must be just as necessarily idealist as realist? Isn't all theology necessarily idealist to the extent that thinking about God's given reality always involves referring to its non-given truth? Doesn't all theology understand the given in light of the immanent reality not given to it?

Idealism does not stand empty-handed before the problem of realism, that is, the problem of immanence. Idealism directs its gaze beyond the stars of heaven or heart to the stars of God. That does not mean heaven and heart are ignored. It means God is the creative logos distinct from all other being. This creative logos is joyfully recognized as the being by which all other being is borne. That is why idealism will not relinquish the concept of revelation. It will insist on its "I desire nothing but God and the soul" as little as did Augustine, the great idealist among the theologians. Nor will it insist on the line, "Call it noise and smoke befogging heaven's glow," but with Goethe will have the humor and condescension to continue:

> Through all things flows the joy for life,
> From the smallest to the greatest star;
> And all that struggles, all that strives,
> Finds rest eternal in God the Lord.

Idealism does not turn the absolute into a death-blow to the relative. It will not turn the unconditioned into an idol that smirks in the face of anyone who thinks only the conditioned is worth taking seriously. All that would only betray a dilettantish idealism, which it would be idle to oppose. Genuine idealism will affirm mysticism, but also culture. It will not only discover and proclaim the self-existent God as the great idea and truth. It will also discover and proclaim that in God all ideas, truths, principles — all practical and theoretical concepts — originate. Although its method is to start with the lonely I in contradistinction to the Thou, in the end it need not minimize the Thou and community with it. Genuine idealism describes a hyperbola. It leads away from reality into the realm of truth (which does not necessarily coincide with reality), but from there it leads back to reality, now understood as the context where truths are found. In its own way genuine idealism does not exclude but includes the given. That is what makes Christian, theological idealism possible: a critical understanding of revelation's givenness.

Crisis does not mean negation. It means chastening the knowledge of the given for the sake of its strengthening — chastening it by rejecting the self-evident status it has for realism; strengthening it by restoring its true connection. Is this possible? As we have said before, it is necessary. Or shouldn't it be necessary to subject revelation to this crisis — revelation conceived of as something given? We certainly saw what reservations are in order when it comes to realism: God is not fate, not nature, not history, not simply there. The Word became flesh, but flesh is not for that reason the Word. The relationship is irreversible. Flesh is the Word only because and only to the extent that the Word became flesh in a particular instance. Given theological realism's presuppositions, one cannot say that these distinctions are unambiguously secured.

Idealism in theology obviously aspires to take all this into consideration. It aspires to do justice to God's hiddenness even in the midst of his revelation, to the divine hiddenness that points to the divine disclosure. Hence where the realist asserts: "God is reality," idealism counters: "God is truth." Hence idealism does not bypass reality, but regards it as transparent, so that through it the truth shines forth; otherwise, it would not be of God. Hence it takes pains to criticize subjective as well as objective experience. Hence, to the annoyance of the realists, it speaks of the figurative or symbolic character of God's objective and subjective givenness. Hence it stresses similarity to God in the midst of even greater dissimilarity.[5] We must not forget that a genuine and necessary aspiration is at stake here. "Great men who recognize so great a God" is how Augustine not unjustly described Plato and the Platonists, in the midst of discussing pre-socratic and especially Ionic philosophy.[6]

No one who wanted to expunge all idealism from theology would be a very sharp Christian theologian, merely a naive realist. Nor should Zwingli and Calvin even more foolishly be decried as humanists, because in relative opposition to Luther and his followers, they thought they had to make these concerns their own. Idealism is the antidote to all demonology passing itself off as theology. By stressing God's non-objectivity it reminds us that all human thinking and speaking about God is inadequate. It protects theology's object from being confused with other objects. It directs us to the God who is God only in genuine transcendence. Theology needs this antidote and this modesty. A theology completely ridded of idealism would be a pagan monstrosity. Classical realism is itself the best witness that in theology at least the second word needs to be that of critical idealism.

Therefore, at this point too we would do well not to dismiss, but to understand. But of course that means some questions need to be raised. The Christianity of idealist theology is not beyond jeopardy. The jeopardy is actually greater than with realism, because from the standpoint of intellectual history, idealism represents a second, more audacious step — a "deeper" possibility of human reflection about God. Demonology might be cast out from theology only to be replaced by ideology, and theology can be just as hard to distinguish from the latter as from the former. To determine idealism's rightful place in theology, we will need some criteria. Above all we will need to reach an understanding with the theological idealist about his hyperbola. We will need to make certain that his critical view of reality as the context where truth is found has nothing to do with a general way to God open and accessible at all times to everyone. That is the idealist's peculiar pride. By referring to the timeless truths of reason, directly accessible to everyone, the idealist brushes aside the realist's accidental and particular truths of history. To theology this pride makes him very suspicious. If theology is to remain grounded in God's revelation, then the idealist is going to have to dampen his ardor for a generally accessible truth, and to join forces with the realist. He is going to have to grant that "accessibility" here can only mean the possibility of God's access to us, not of our access to God. He will also have to join forces with the realist by granting that God's truth finds access to us in one single particular event and that this event is definitive. If his hyperbola is not to be an empty scheme, he will have to concede that in himself he possesses no criterion by which to distinguish truth from reality, but that this criterion must be given to him in and with revelation itself. He will therefore have to regard revelation as a possibility specific to God, not as a general human possibility. In fact, as a Christian theologian he will have to regard it as the divine possibility actualized in Christ, or in the biblical and ecclesiastical witness to Christ. He will have to admit that neither human reason in general and as such, nor the phenomenon of nature and history in general and as such, can be proclaimed as organs, witnesses or symbols of revelation. He will need to realize that only where the Word of God — which is bound neither to our reason nor to worldly phenomena — gives it sense, does his critical analysis make sense. And as a Christian theologian he will need to be clear about just how concretely and in just what connection he must ask about this sense. In this light it may be said that Augustine and Calvin, who placed themselves under rather than over the Word, were idealist theologians.

A second issue needs to be raised with the theological idealist. Assume that his hyperbola, his critique of reality, has a bearing on God's revelation. The critique operates with a human conceptual scheme. It uses dialectical modes of thought to play of God's givenness against his non-givenness in his revelation. No more than a copy of the reality of God's truth or the truth of God's reality can result from this procedure. Never can it be a substitute for God's Word. Consider, for example, the idealist theologian, A. E. Biedermann. Through a thorough-going process of abstraction, he thinks he can trace the biblical and ecclesiastical "image" back to the "pure concept." He thinks he can present in human words what is essential, what is really meant — by God. In such a case one must ask whether — quite contrary to idealist intentions — the human logos has not simply been confused with the divine. The question becomes even more urgent in the case of A. Ritschl, whose theology rests on a rather primitive contrast between spirit and nature. He seems to have forgotten completely that the spiritual realm, no less than the natural, has creaturely status, and that as such it therefore gives us no access to God. Schleiermacher, on the other hand, knew that God is to be sought beyond this inner-worldly contrast. That alone shows how vastly superior he was to that other theological master from the previous century; and that alone makes him worth attending to, even if one cannot say this insight bore fruit in his theology.

Therefore, the idealist theologian must be asked whether he agrees with us about the transcendence of God to which he would point us. Isn't it something different that the self-transcendence of our own created and fallen spirits? Isn't it something more than merely the relative uncertainty of our own spiritual life? Isn't it rather the very transcendence of the Creator who made heaven and earth, nature and spirit, "all things visible and invisible"? Aren't we therefore better off by not assuming we can adequately reproduce God's Word? Doesn't our task require — in the best sense of idealism — respect for the boundaries of human existence? Isn't our task simply to serve, set forth and bear witness to God's Word through the dialectic of human concepts?

Theology is certainly intellectual work, but its object of inquiry is neither spirit nor nature, and therefore strictly speaking it belongs just as little to the humanities as to the sciences. Its object is the Word dwelling in inapproachable light. Theology neither produces nor articulates it. It bears witness to it. Nor does it do this by some sort of trick that could also be done by Pharaoh's magicians. It does this, rather, by virtue of the Word's having come to us, of its having a church, of its having issued a call through God's action in a particular event. Theology answers this call. It neither re-issues, nor replaces, nor proposes to be God's Word itself. It merely copies and in so doing does not claim to be accomplishing the creative work. It does not claim its dialectic as the meaning toward which it aims. When this claim is dropped, the idealist can be a theologian.

A third question must be posed to the idealist. Would he agree that when knowledge of God is at stake, the truth is substantiated by God's action — not by God's action along with ours, but by God's action alone? Knowledge of God in his Word is the knowledge of faith. Yet faith understands its knowledge as given by God — not as a human work, nor as divine and human collaboration, but as our being known by God's Word. Probably the toughest question facing the idealist, but not one he can be spared, is this: When it comes to knowledge of God, is he willing to abandon the notion of "tension" between divine and human action? For how does one come to speak of "tension" at this point anyway, of an action "at once divine and human"? Doesn't that simply confuse knowledge of God with some other kind of knowledge? This "at once," this "at the same time," is in fact characteristic of all other knowledge. The familiar antithesis between spontaneity and receptivity remains valid there.

Since the only thought available to us is human thought, even when it comes to knowledge of God, we won't be able to avoid using this antithesis. Our use of it, however, can only be regulative, not constitutive. By means of ordinary scholarly inquiry (and thus in the form of discursive knowledge), theology is called to discuss knowledge that is not discursive, and in which that antithesis does not occur. When the Reformers described faith as "a strictly passive matter" (*res mere passiva*), they did not mean that faith included only one aspect of rational activity — receptivity but not spontaneity. There is no receptivity without spontaneity as well, and faith cannot of course be reduced to some sort of trance-like condition. No, reason's normal activity is not interrupted; but it is directed, guided and ordered by something superior to itself, something that has no part in its antithesis. Taken as a whole (as activity spontaneous and receptive), reason is passively related to that superior reality. It is related to it, in other words, obediently. That is the oddity about knowledge of God as compared with other knowledge. To implicate this superior reality, to which we are obedient, in the antithesis between spontaneity and receptivity would be senseless.[7] When we are dealing with the knowledge of things, this antithesis is in force. There we enter the realm of never-ending tensions where Burdian's may decide who is to be king. There all roles are interchangeable. There above can mean below, and below can mean above, as shown by the way Hegelian idealism suddenly changed into the materialism of the second half of the previous century.

The reason why God is not to be sought in reason, and not to be confused with created spirit, is that created spirit does not know itself except in terms of that antithesis. It knows itself only in contrast to something outside itself. A tension certainly exists between the two, but created spirit is not then related to something unambiguously superior. To equate reason with God (*ratio sive Deus*) is just as intolerable as to equate nature with God (*natura sive Deus*). Faith believes in neither — neither in created spirit nor in the external reality by which spirit knows itself. Faith does not believe in these mutually limiting realities. It does not believe in the sort of unconditionality that is unconditioned only in contrast to conditioned reality, and whose relationship is therefore reversible.

Faith believes in the Creator of all things and thereby in no further object. It believes in the One who is Lord over those "objects" *natura* and *ratio*, who is therefore the origin not only of their being there, but also of their being over against each other. Since faith is knowledge of the Creator, not knowledge of some existing object in the antithesis previously mentioned, it follows that faith is not the kind of knowledge in which we can see ourselves as creative. In this knowledge we must rather see ourselves as obedient. Its truth can only be apprehended in one way — as the truth that is said to us. Anything we might say to ourselves in this regard must always begin and end with obedience, and obedience cannot be grounded in anything but the truth said to us. Obedience must here be pure obedience. Only under one condition is this possible and conceivable — that the God who really is God (and not just our idea of God) has spoken to us.

Anything said about this God can be said only as a matter of obedience, never mind its being set forth in the form of objective human knowledge, in the same framework as philosophical discourse, under the constraint of the same dialectical movement. It can only rest on God's having spoken, not on our having said something to ourselves. There can be no question of reciprocity between God's action and our own. It is strictly a matter of the command in which we know our obedience to be grounded. We have not proven that such a command exists. We will take care to refrain from doing so. We can only establish that on the basis of this command theology speaks of God. In this case that is how the truth is ascertained. Should it be said that ascertaining this truth is divinely and humanly accomplished, then the terms of discussion are no longer being set by faith and hearing the Word. The idealists don't really mean idea, do they, when they talk of God? For if they did, then we would be forced to say of them what Irenaeus said of the Gnostics: "Speaking things resembling the [doctrine of the] faithful. . .not only do they hold opinions which are different, but absolutely contrary, and in all points full of blasphemies." And: "Lime is wickedly mixed with the milk of God."[8]

III

Theology operates in the same context as philosophy. It must, however, attend to its own affairs. Nonetheless, as it develops its own material, it cannot escape the problem of philosophy. Theology too must come to terms with the two boundaries of human thought — truth and reality. In God's countenance the very traits of fate and idea seem to be displayed. Certainly theology cannot pursue its calling without trying to think dialectically about how God is given and not given at the same time. We have seen that theology can be predominately realist or predominately idealist. We have noted dangerous approximations to pure realism and pure idealism. In the one case theology is blurred with natural science, in the other with the humanities. Demonology results from the first blurring, ideology from the second. We have also observed how with equal strength a corrective tends to arise in each case. The material itself apparently requires each to deal with the other's concern. Each side seems impelled to bring the other's opposing thesis somehow under its own denominator.

All this takes place with parallels and connections to what happens in philosophy. Although theology pursues its own affairs within the same context, that does not guarantee that, whether realistically or idealistically oriented, it will actually develop an inclusion of its opposite type. Yet it is possible that like a good philosophy of either kind, theology will not fail to include its opposite dialectically. That does not yet make it good theology. Whether it is good theology or not depends on how this inclusion is brought about, not on the inclusion itself. In philosophy such an inclusion always means proposing and promoting, or at least attempting, a synthesis — that is, some third postulate superior to the two opposites. To that extent the realist makes a crucial concession to the idealist, and vice versa. For each would claim — what philosophy has not? — that from its own standpoint the dualism of the two boundaries can be surveyed, criticized and ultimately overcome.

What kind of philosophy would it be that didn't strive to see things as a whole, even if when describing the whole it were so cautious as to resort to drawing merely a dotted line when it came to the decisive arc? With identical emphasis and confidence, the one philosopher will find the superior and reconciling principle in "being," while the other will find it in "logos." Truth will be a predicate of reality for the one, while for the other, reality will be a predicate of truth. Although the two philosophers part company by deciding one way or the other, they find themselves all the more together by advancing a synthesis, a superior and reconciling principle. They thereby reveal themselves as philosophical (which is to say, non-theological) thinkers.

Would it make one a theologian if one knew how, as realist or idealist, to think beyond this contrast and to make one's *primum* or *secundum* valid as a *tertium*? What philosophy could then escape being claimed as essentially theology? Do theology's credentials depend, with all due discretion, on its success in producing its *primum* or *secundum* as a superior and reconciling *tertium* — as widely claimed on the realist side by virtue of a Thomas, and on the idealist side by virtue of a Hegel? Things are not, however, so easy. To practice the art of synthesis is philosophy's right and is not as such to be challenged by theology. Yet even if it were to risk far less than Thomas and Hegel, even if it were to proceed with the self-possession (one might just as well say the cultured enthusiasm) of a Kant, what philosophy would not have to see in the very quest for synthesis at least its esoteric secret, perhaps even its insoluble problem? Philosophical dialectic at least aspires to say an ultimately definitive word, at least aims in that direction, at least considers it to be potentially utterable.

Good for it, if at the same time it remains conscious of its limits as philosophy, as reflection on the reality and truth of human existence, at whose limits the idea of God can emerge only as a question. Good for it, if it does not confuse the theological problem of how to speak positively about God with its own problem, but sees the former in its peculiarity, if it at least sees the necessity of respecting it in its own way. Good for it, if it therefore does not step forward as disguised theology, ersatz theology, theosophy, if it does not confuse the synthesis it proposes, promotes, or in any case approximates, with God. Theology will then have no objection to raise against this, the philosophical way of thinking dialectically about the contradiction.

If theology itself wants to make use of dialectic, however, it has to mean something else if it is not to surrender its proper concern. Theology may be oriented toward realism or idealism, but as theology it has neither the *primum* nor the *secundum* as an overarching *tertium*. It has no *tertium* at all — neither to propose and promote, nor to suggest, nor even to approximate. The art of theology cannot be the art of synthesis. It may practice the art of including the opposite dialectically. To that extent it may even be addressed as philosophy. But it must distinguish itself as *philosophia sacra* from all philosophy, and from classical philosophy as embodied in Thomas and Hegel most of all. That is, it must refrain from all reaching — however ingeniously, piously or covertly — for a grand synthesis of opposites.

Why is that? Because theology is in no sense to be anthropology. Because instead of reflecting on the reality and truth of human existence, it reflects on the reality and truth of God's Word as spoken to human existence. Theology does not take pains to think dialectically about opposites because of the contradiction in human thought (which intimates a contradiction in human existence). This contradiction does not pose a riddle for which, as a technical discipline supposedly focused on humanity (say, humanity as it reflects on its own existence), it would more or less know how to give a clear and definite answer. On the contrary, theology thinks dialectically, because this contradiction has been placed into the world of thought and existence by God's Word as something it and only it resolves. Theology must therefore set out from the point at which philosophy thinks it can arrive or at least would like to arrive. Moreover, theology claims that this very point can only be given in advance, that reflection on God can only proceed in the form of a thinking from rather than a thinking toward. It must reject the claim that one might just as well arrive at this point by reflecting on the reality and truth of human existence — if by "this point" we mean an ultimate word, a naming of God worthy of the name.

Between theology and a philosophy that strictly remains philosophy, what can and will exist is not only a well-wishing neutrality, not only concord but — at least for the theology in whose name we speak here — a rich and instructive community of work. War, however, and indeed war to the knife, is what can and will exist between theology and every philosophy which, by whatever pretext, wants to be theosophy. The reason is that theology has to regard human beings as creatures of illusion when in the course of self-reflection (be it ever so existentiell; be it even the self-reflection of the "I" addressed by the "Thou"), they think they can discover an ultimate word in their own sphere, when they think they can really discover God in action through human self-reflection. As we now remind ourselves for the third time, it is the concept of sin, of fallen humanity, which we have had to bring to bear against realism and idealism.

Any *tertium* beyond reality and truth that one might propose and promote, or suggest and approximate, is not and never can be God. Thus runs the negative thesis to be advanced here. As a preliminary confirmation of this thesis, one might argue that up to now no Philosophy has ever succeeded in making even conceptually clear a genuine *tertium* beyond these oppositions. Instead, even in the best of cases we are offered, godlike and triumphant, a splendid but also suspicious one-sidedness, the predominance of a *primum* or a *secundum*: *esse* or *nosse*, *nosse* or *esse* (being or knowing, knowing or being). Nonetheless, we do not want to base our negative theology on the ultimate failure, which is probably obvious, of the art of philosophical synthesis, that is to say, on an argument from ignorance. Instead, we would simply base it on a question. Would the person of faith, to whom God has been revealed through his Word, consider even for a moment ascribing to himself any knowledge of God apart from Word and faith? Wouldn't he have to deny possessing any capacity for this knowledge? Wouldn't he have to say that insofar as he took fate and idea to be his God, he was still pursuing idols of his own making, deified "principalities, powers and dominions"? Wouldn't he have to say his natural religion of salvation was related to faith not as a useful prelude or preparation, but as darkness to light, as death to life? Between the God we conceive for ourselves and the God known through his Word, between God the earnestly desired and satisfying conclusion to our self-reflection and God as actually given to us, what else could possibly exist for faith than decision, and either/or? Where the synergistic picture holds sway in which "natural" knowledge of God is agreeably completed by revealed knowledge, what other result can there be than that theology has given itself up as theology — surrendered its character as a theology of revelation and faith?

We can now perhaps grasp what Luther had in mind when he warned so vigorously against *speculatio majestatis*. By that he meant speculating about "God in his incomprehensible power, wisdom, and majesty." Any such enterprise he immediately associated with the works righteousness of monks by which they interposed "works, fasts, cowl, and tonsure" between themselves and God. They who do "not know the doctrine of justification" — they are the ones who do that, who pursue natural theology. "If you attempt to comprehend God in this way . . . you will inevitably fall, as Lucifer did, and in horrible despair lose God and everything." "Whoever investigates the majesty of God will be consumed by his glory." For "in his own nature" God is absolutely "intolerable to human nature"[9] (even, wrote Luther, to the human body). When pondering these words one cannot help but think of the "numinous" that Rudolf Otto not only described in his book on "the holy," but also rendered so commendably in all its diabolical grotesquery, as though in effigy. That is fate! That is idea!

If it is difficult for us to share the revulsion Luther felt toward this God, if it is not clear how semi-pelagianism could be the mortal danger it is made out to be here, if we suppose that we don't have to take the doctrine of justification seriously, then none of that speaks against Luther but against us. If we human beings are sinners lost and condemned, and if as such we wad up the reality and truth of our existence into an ultimate word and call that ultimate word God, then how could the majesty imagined of this God be anything other than the *majestas Diaboli*? This particular "wholly other" — the one that is only our mirror image, the keystone in the arches of our culture and for that reason no "wholly other" at all, but simply the last in a long line of human works — this wholly other can be nothing for us but judgment without grace. For precisely when we want to find God in it, believing we have spoken our ultimate word, we remain alone with ourselves, shut up in our prison of distance, alienation and hostility toward God. That is why the cult of any God won through dialectics is monkish legalism, indeed a fatal legalism, no less than any other. To want to speak a human word at the very point where everything depends on letting God's Word be spoken, is fatal "self-assertion" *(seipsum interponere)*. Theology must therefore resist the impulse to devise a grand synthesis of opposites.

Since theology means something other than a humanly proposed *tertium* beyond truth and reality, it cannot evade the task of conceptualizing God. Since it sets forth from the very point at which philosophy qua theosophy thinks it can arrive, theology must also, if it is not to bog down in prolegomena, actually speak about God. It must therefore run risks — the risk of misunderstanding, as though it too were pursuing theosophy, or the even greater risk of lapsing into theosophy unawares. Although it has often been overlooked, Luther despite his warning did not reject the necessity of theological dialectic. "When you leave the doctrine of justification" *(extra justificationem)*, in other words, when there is no question of devising one's own God, then the task is simply to say to "Jews, Turks, or sectarians, etc." what one means in contrast to them when one utters the word "God." In this sense Luther thought that referring to God "in his nature" was quite appropriate, and he knew that then theology too had to bring into play the otherwise despised art of *speculatio majestatis*. "Then you must use all your cleverness and effort and be as subtle and crafty a debater as possible"![10]

By setting out to speak of God, theology must travel down the same road as philosophy, even though in the opposite direction. In our detailed comments on the realist and idealist possibilities, we have seen to what extent, how far. Will it, and how will it, travel down this road without reproach? The necessity and possibility of theological dialectic can all too easily become a trojan horse in whose belly the noxious enemy of old nonetheless enters into Illium. As Luther himself has shown, Erasmus can only be contested with Erasmian weapons, and that means theological dialectic. But who can guarantee that in the thick of things the courageous dialectician — if he is not exactly named Luther — will not become a little Erasmus himself? Who can protect even our best concept of God from degenerating — not only in the eyes of others, but also in our own — into a deified concept that once again wreaks havoc with the doctrine of justification?

These unavoidable risks will caution the theologian against hastily accusing others of having done theosophy instead of theology. When it comes to others — whether a Thomas or a Schleiermacher or a Biedermann — we can do no more than raise questions. What do we really know? What do we know even when it comes to the philosophers? Do we really know whether they are chasing after the phantasm of a "naked God" (*Deus nudus*) attained by "rational investigation" (*judicio rationis*)? Do we really know whether their thinking merely heads toward the point from which we believe ours must set forth, whether theirs is not at least as good if not better than our own? Is it clear to us how easily we ourselves can be caught in the act of not setting forth from that point? Even in the case of Luther contra Erasmus there is of course some doubt whether Luther, in pursuing the *speculatio majestatis* (which he too engaged in), set forth entirely from that point. As "subtle and crafty debaters" who pursue natural theology quite deftly and vulgarly, is it clear how readily we are drawn to think in the opposite direction, not from the point but toward it? Although overtly engaged in busy theological activity, is it clear how boldly we publish the God of human synthesis, the deified concept?

If we see clearly, we will not reject the possibility that in others' speculation (which we perhaps justly find so irritating) and despite all the doubtfulness of its course (and why shouldn't we think of the philosophers here among others?), something of the knowledge of God by and in his Word might come through. Theological reality, in our case and theirs, might always be as mixed and ambiguous as reality in general. In that very situation it would have to be made clear that the unity of reality and truth occurs in and only in God's Word. It would also have to be made clear that we do not confuse our own theological reality with the truth, and therefore that we do not mistake the theological reality of others, sometimes apparently so fatal, for untruth.

We can and must ask each other very rigorous questions. "How do you thus bring sin to bear on these considerations?" (*Cogitasi quanti ponderis sit peccatum*?) Is it really valid to claim the following: That the *tertium* is strictly and exclusively God's and not our own? That this *tertium* can certainly be an object of faith but not of knowledge? That all our dialectic must claim and presuppose this *tertium* without ever once getting a bead on it, to say nothing of holding it in view? Do we well know that faith, by which alone God is known and can be spoken of, is not a daring human leap, but simply obedience? We will, however, ask each other these things all the more rigorously, the more rigorously we have questioned ourselves in advance, and the more we remain open to being questioned in return. For a conclusive judgment about the other, for a theology that is strictly correct, for a history of theology in which the sheep can really be separated from the goats, there obviously isn't enough to go on, nor should there be.

To determine whether a particular theology has as its object merely a deified concept or the living God, the first criterion might be whether this theology is conscious of its own relativity. Has it retained the patience necessary toward other theologies (which is quite compatible with posing rigorous questions)? A theology too impatient in polemics might just be a theology of the *Deus nudus*. A theology based on God's Word, at any rate, will need to be patient as well as incisive. For God is indeed patient, and with whom does he need to exercise more patience on this sorry earth than with us theologians, never mind what variety.

The theoretical background to this practical criterion is the conception of free divine election. We thus cannot boast to others about our hearing the Word. In hearing the Word we stand either by obedience or we do not stand at all. For not only the Word's being spoken but also our reception of it is always a matter of God's free grace. It is therefore not a matter in which one might adopt a so-called standpoint by which to exalt oneself over others. If I happen to be right instead of them, then so be it, but no triumph here will ever be mine. It will be God's alone, any possible triumph on my part quickly receding into the shadows from which it came. God's Word is not bound, nor ever will be bound. Theological dialectic can be genuine only as it is open to this conception—only as it serves this and only this conception, that is, as it serves the freedom of God's Word.

God's Word means God's election. A real theology of God's Word is therefore not the sort of thing one can take or leave. So conceived, the theology of God's Word would always be a natural, philosophical theology, one more possibility among others. Real theology of God's Word is the sort of thing by which one can only be taken or left. It gets underway only if, no, only when God is underway "with his Spirit and gifts." But God's Spirit blows where it will. If I am called to do this theology, then so I am. Not because I found a way to God, but because God found a way to me. Not because I bind myself to God, but because God binds me to himself. Not because my dialectics are so great, but because God condescends to make use of me and this my doubtful tool. Therefore, not because I have unearthed the tablets of wisdom or squared the circle or discovered the magic point at which reality and truth intersect. Not because I can demonstrate how fate is really idea, or idea really fate, or how my synthesis of them is really God; but rather because it has pleased God, as the one superior to the contradiction of my existence and my thought, to step in for me as Revealer and Reconciler so that I should confess him; and therefore because it has pleased God to confess himself to me.

In itself and as such how could my God-concept ever be a witness to God? It can, however, please God to make it be that and to use it in that way. These then are the terms on which I may and must risk being a theologian — in obedience, equipped with these powers of my thought. It would simply be impossible to be a theologian, that is, from the standpoint of faith, if one were not allowed and in fact compelled to take risks on these terms.

A second theoretical criterion for a theology of God's Word thereby commends itself. Theology will only be a theology of God's Word if it somehow makes the concept of predestination central to its concept of God instead of regarding it as just one among others. A theology ignorant that even its best concept of God, informed by the pinnacle of human thought, is in itself no witness to God can only be, strictly speaking, a witness to the devil. With the most subtle and pious dialectical movement between the concepts fate and idea, theology may still be tempted to capture God in a theory. It may still try to set up a system, to close the circle, or to think it has closed the circle, when in fact all it can ever do is to draw out radii continually from the center. It may suppose it has grasped the Spirit with its word, and the Word with its spirit. It may even make out the dogma of predestination to be a harmless little token of how we appropriate salvation instead of — precisely because that is indeed at stake — placing it at the forefront of all its deliberations with the vigor of the old Reformed dogmaticians. When theology moves in these directions, it ought to suspect that it is engaged in *speculatio majestatis* of the *Deus nudus*, in *theologia gloria* instead of *theologia crucis*, as Luther once said in another place.

Even for theology there is no other justification than justification by faith. Or, to put it another way, theology is justified only by obedience. For even obedience can be obedience only when it understands itself as faith — as the human affirmation of God's free, unearned, unowed and uncompelled grace. Theology, too, must do its work in appropriate humility. And we say nothing different if we remember in conclusion that Luther put the decisive contradiction to all *speculatio majestatis* like this: ". . . begin where Christ began — in the Virgin's womb, in the manger, and at his mother's breasts." Begin, in other words, where God's Word has and does concretely come to us: In truth, because it is God's Word. In reality, because it was made flesh. True God and real humanity — in just that way, the one, the divine, the binding, the justifying and sanctifying Word. Theology will really be theology — of Word, election, faith — when from beginning to end it is christology.

Footnotes

1. *Summa Theologicae* I, 1. 7.

2 Cf. the exemplary and cautious definition of the relationship between theology and philosophy as set forth by Aquinas, *Summa contra Gentiles* II, 4.

3. Martin Luther, *Lectures on Galatians 1535* in *Luther's Works*, Vol. 26 (St. Louis: Concordia Publishing House, 1963), p. 171.

4. *Summa Theologicae* I, 12, 13.

5. The Fourth Lateran Council (1215) in Denzinger, *The Sources of Catholic Dogma* (St. Louis: Herder, 1957), par. 432, p. 171.

6. *De civitate Dei* VIII, 5.

7. This confusion occurs, for example, in H. Stephan, *Glaubenslehre*, second edition (1928), p. 44f.

8. *Against Heresies* III, 17. 4.

9. Luther, *op. cit.*, p. 87. (Unless otherwise indicated, any further quotations from Luther in Barth's text are from this passage. —Tr.)

10 *Ibid.*, p. 88.

—Translated by George Hunsinger

KARL BARTH
The First Commandment as an Axiom of Theology

An *axiom* is a statement which cannot be proven by other statements. Indeed it is not in need of being proven by other statements. It proves itself. It is a statement which is sufficiently comprehensive and substantial to form the ultimate and decisive presupposition to the proof of all other statements of a particular scientific discipline. If there is also an axiom of *theology*, as the title of this address implies, then what is meant is this: theology too rests in regard to the proof of its statements on an ultimate and decisive presupposition. As such, it can neither be proven nor is it in need of proof. It contains in itself everything which is necessary for its proof. It can be stated just as the axiom or axioms of any other discipline. The statements of theology are measured by the axiom every bit as rigorously as the statements of every other discipline are measured by its axioms. Thus every theology is subject to the statements; i.e., whether and how it can be proven by the axiom and, therefore, whether and how it is tenable and legitimate.

But then, anyone speaking of an axiom of *theology* and even specifying that it is the *first commandment* - the familiar first commandment of the Decalogue - must understand from the outset that this concept is being given a content and a meaning which it can have only in theology. In no way must it be assumed that the choice of this concept has provided a common platform, a "point of contact" for dialogue with logicians, mathematicians and physicists. One must not be surprised when logicians, mathematicians and physicists criticize this choice as an intolerable misuse of this concept. One will know, even before this criticism is made, that the presupposition of theology, the first commandment, is an instance *sui generis*. Indeed, the concept "axiom" will not be chosen to describe that instance because it is believed that the first commandment can be subsumed under this concept. Nor will the concept be chosen because one can discern an intrinsic similarity or an imminent analogy to the first commandment - and thus provide the ability to understand it. The concept will not be chosen, therefore, because of its suitability. We assert that it is not *through* the concept axiom," but only *by means of* it (to be precise, *in spite of* it, only by trespassing on its customary usage, even reversing it, only by a misuse of this concept) can we designate the presupposition for theology and its significance for theological statements.

What applies to all elements of human language, be they part of the philosophical or any other sphere, applies equally to the concept "axiom." The concept itself contains *nothing* analogous to what it connotes in its theological use. The most one can say is that this use of the concept may perhaps be *given* this analogy, this "likeness of faith" (Romans 12:6). By virtue of this received analogy (but certainly not by virtue of any inherent analogy), the concept "axiom" may indeed serve as a "point of contact" for a discussion about the presupposition of theology.

If the first commandment should be in fact the presupposition of all theology, then the following conclusion (which necessarily arises out of this equation and in the light of which we can immediately clarify for ourselves the meaning of this equation) must emphatically be stated before anything else. Whatever "axiom" means here must be determined by the matter which it designates in this discussion irrespective of the general sense of that concept.

"You shall have no other gods before me.!" Theology is in no position to make a binding acknowledgment of the meaning proper to language at any one point. It cannot possibly allow language to become the master. We say "axiom" because, in this concept, an opportunity to try to say just what the concept in its general use could *not* say - namely, what this absolutely fundamental and foundational presupposition of theology is all about.

The reverse is equally true. Whoever would really hear what we are trying to assert will not hear what is the customary use of the concept. Indeed, through the misuse of the concept, one is offered an opportunity to hear what one could not possibly hear were the concept used in the normal sense.

I shall speak first of the special content, the special meaning, which the concept "axiom" acquires when it designates the presupposition of theology.

1. The first commandment *"is written"* in Exodus 20. It is essential to the axiom of theology that it "is written," that it is part of the document in relation to which the church exists as the church in the world. The church exists in her reading and proclaiming this document as the unique

witness of God's unique revelation, in reading, proclaiming and reading again, proclaiming, reading and proclaiming again. In this movement of life of the church, theology also exists. For that reason, the statements of theology basically can be only interpretation. When we speak here and now of no other than the first commandment, we identify a quite specific passage of that document. We believe that there we hear very clearly the axiom of theology.

Of course, we could hear it in other passages in the document. We could cite as the axiom of theology John 1:16 ("The Word became flesh, he dwelt among us, and we beheld his glory") or Matthew 11:28 ("Come to me, all who labour and are heavy laden") or 2 Corinthians 5:19 ("God was in Christ reconciling the world to himself"). All these verses tell us basically what the first commandment tells us. Nothing is said in first commandment that is not also said in those versions in their own manner and in their own context. If we had ears to hear, every page of that document would speak to us of the one presupposition of theology. Yet the relation in which the church exists, its relation to that document, must always be a relation to a quite specific place in that document. It must be a relation to a specific "text" which speaks to the church at whatever the time and in whatever the place as *pars pro toto*. We are trying here and now to let that passage, the first commandment, speak to us as an axiom of theology.

It should be clear by now that we have transcended the general meaning of "axiom" merely by raising the question of the axiom of theology within the sphere of the church. For that reason, obviously, we have found the answer precisely in that document. It should not be essential to axioms, in the general meaning of the term, that they should "be written" somewhere in a specific authoritative document. Rather, they should be directly, immediately and generally perceivable. They should be persuasive without any formal authority, regardless of whether or where they are written.

The first commandment, the theological axiom, however, is not perceivable in a direct, immediate or general way. It is an axiom only because and insofar as it "is written". It is written for a church for which it has authority and which exists by, and only by, reading and proclaiming this written word.

2. The first commandment is written as a report about an *event in time*, namely as words addressed by one person to another. "And the Lord God spoke all these words, saying 'I am the Lord *your* god. *You*

shall have no other gods before *me!*" I-Thou! God appears! In this address the axiom of theology is established. Whatever we think that we know about God's eternity, it must not cause us to erase even one iota from the character of this axiom as an event, not if we want to understand anything at all here. There is not talk of a timeless *relation* between humanity and God, but of a *history* which occurs in time.

Thinking *sub specie aeterni* is of no use at all here. Even in the book of Exodus it is meant that the word became flesh, that God speaks to human beings in human language, in the ways of human existence and, therefore, in time. We understand the axiom of theology, not by trying to capture the timeless meaning of this temporal event, but by becoming *contemporary* with this temporal event through the hearing of the written first commandment. The axiom of theology is understood only by the person who in his or her own time has to deal with the same temporally determined address of God which the Israelites at Sinai in their time had to deal with for better or for worse. In no way can one understand that temporal event as if one were a spectator or an arbiter.

Obviously one cannot say of an axiom in the *general* sense of the term that *its* truth and validity are tied to such an address, such an I-Thou event, such a happening in time. It cannot be mediated at all through a person to person address. It is known immediately or not at all. It becomes evident through itself. It is timelessly evident and it is quite independent of the event of its perception. The event, history, can be only a "medium," as it was said in the eighteenth century.

Wherever allegedly ultimate truths are *independent* in that way, wherever they are based on themselves, *abstracted* from persons and from time, we are dealing with axioms in the general sense of the word, even when they claim to be religious or christian truth. We are not dealing then with the axiom of theology. This axiom is recognized by virtue of its reality and validity in the moment, the temporal moment of its revelation from person to person. It is, therefore, a thought determined and bound by that moment. It is the eternity of the Word which, as it is written, has concealed itself and still continues to do so in human flesh and therefore in time.

3. If it is to be understood in its biblical context, the first commandment and therefore the axiom of theology can be understood as it comes to us, namely as a *commandment*. Essentially it is not only something God says about himself, perhaps about God's uniqueness or that there are no other gods before God. It is not only a revelation of divine truth.

It is essentially a *command* of God to the Israelite who is personally addressed. God not only *designates* himself as lord but *acts* as such by demanding, commanding and forbidding: "You shall have no other gods before me!"

Nothing may be abstracted from this divine behaviour, this factual lordship of God. The axiom of theology is in essence the establishment of a divine position. Therefore human cognition of the axiom of theology is also essentially qualified as the establishment of a definite position. If we do not hear what is being said to us, it means not only that we are mistaken but also that we are disobedient. If we hear what is being said to us it means that we have not only rightly understood but also that we are obedient. It means first and foremost obedience or disobedience. The divine truth, which is, of course, also spoken to us through the commandment, comes to us (if it comes to us) through a divine *decision* and through a *human* decision which responds to it in one way or another.

However, this description is also alien to the general concept of axiom. In order to be understood, an axiom in the general sense needs no divine commandment. Neither is the fact of its cognition or non-cognition to be spoken of as obedience or disobedience. Instead the axiom in the general sense waits somewhere in the sphere of the human, to be discovered and valued by human beings. (Whether the axiom waits in things themselves or in human reason is a question to be left to the philosophers.) It receives and has validity for us, it is *axioma*, in the act of valuation which is basically possible for every human being. Its validity is a triumph of human freedom.

The truth of the axiom of theology, however, lies in the divine sphere and, for that reason its validity is a triumph of divine freedom and a matter of human obedience or disobedience. By recognizing and acknowledging the validity of an axiom in the general sense of the term, I put into practice my dignity as a human being. I risk this ultimate presupposition and push ahead here to the boundaries of humanness. When I acknowledge the validity of the axiom of theology then I acknowledge (not in the realization of my dignity as a human being, but in its limitation which happens to me in that event) that I myself am the object of a presupposition. There *I* am lord. Here I *have* a lord.

Let this be well understood. I not only know that there is a lord. I not only know it, but have one. I have a lord by God's commanding and by my obeying. Indeed, I have a lord also when I do not obey. I have one then in the way that a disobedient servant has a lord. If we wished to have the axiom of theology in another manner — other than as a command issued, one to which we are obedient or disobedient — we would not have it as it is written. We would surely not have the axiom of theology, but an axiom of some other kind.

An essential characteristic of the first commandment is that God who gives this commandment and who takes the title "Lord" is related to the recipient of the commandment as a *liberator* to the liberated, as a *saviour* to the saved. "I am the Lord your god, who brought you out of the land of Egypt, out of the house of bondage." Even this preliminary statement to the commandments is not accidental. From it, nothing can be abstracted. Who this god is, who personally makes his appearance with his command in the first commandment, emerges quite decisively from this preliminary statement to the commandments. He is the redeemer of Israel and thus of every individual Israelite. In his freedom (and we must say quite clearly, in the freedom of his mercy) he chose Israel from among the nations. God has established a covenant with Israel and has, on his part, kept and proven this covenant. Israel exists by virtue of this covenant which was established and kept by its god. The god of the first commandment is, in other words, the god of the human beings who he addresses in the first commandment because God is, and as God is, the mighty and merciful god of Israel.

In Calvin's words, God is the *deus ecclesiae* (Inst. II 8, 14). As such, God says "I and thou." As such God takes the title "Lord" and acts as lord. God was present already in the miraculous act towards a miserable and lost people, a people who in no way deserved to be the people of this god. God had made himself known already, in Luther's words, as "one who is a spring eternal which overflows with sheer goodness, and from which flows everything which is good and which is called good." (WA 30 I, 136, 1).

That is when and why God appears with the commandment. Not for an instant does the law stand by itself, on itself, alone. It stands in and on the good news of God's help in death, which in turn is the promise of further help. "I am the Lord *your* god." *Your* god — the god who has already acted towards you as god — commands: "You shall have no other gods before me!"

"Forget not all his benefits" (Psalm 103:2). To speak of obedience to this commandment is to speak of this not-forgetting. To speak of disobedience to the commandment is to speak of forgetting God's benefits. Obedience is thankfulness. Disobedience is thanklessness. The axiom of theology cannot be separated from this soteriological or, to be quite concrete, from this christological context. Revelation takes place in reconciliation, in the covenant between God and humanity which is established and kept by God. It takes place through forgiveness of sin, justification and sanctification, even as revelation of the law! *Jesus Christ* is the meaning of the law of Sinai inasmuch as he is the revelation of God.

The general meaning of "axiom" fails here completely. What should the truth and knowledge of a logical and mathematical axiom have to do with divine election, covenant making, grace and forgiveness of sin? It is clearly not an axiom because of, and in the death and resurrection of Jesus. It is essential to it to have *no* such preliminary statements. Instead it is true at all times and in all places. Its truth can be known by its own power and significance, by its own right, quite apart from God(s) mercy or anger and with no relation to human salvation or perdition.

One can obviously say similar things about certain axioms basic to the history of morality and politics. They are claimed with a peculiar zeal by contemporary theology as "orders of creation." The axiom of theology however is valid and becomes known in the *regnum gratiae* and exactly because of that, in the church where the proclamation of that kingdom is heard, believed and preached. An axiom which is believed to be abstractly discernible in creation is, whatever else it may be, not the commandment of God and not the commandment of *theology*. This axiom is the word God speaks to his own, those whom he elects and calls. *Subest locutioni relatio* (Calvin I.C).

The first commandment states: *"You shall have no other gods before me!"* What does that mean? What are "other gods"? According to Luther's explanation, which coincides exactly with the biblical view, a god is that in which human beings place their trust, in which they have faith, from which they expect to receive what they love and to protect them from what they fear. A god is that to which one gives one's heart. Luther went on to say that money and possessions, art, wisdom, power, favour, friendship and honour could in this sense as equally well be real gods as the idols of the heathen, the saints of the papacy and, last but not least, our good deeds and our moral achievements. Wherever the human heart is, in other words wherever is the foundation of our real ultimate confidence and hope, the *primum movens* of our vitality and the basis of the security of our lives, there also, in all truth, is our god.

The commandment does not say that there are no other gods beside the one who gives the commandment. Rather it says (and this is something different) that only by *prohibiting* the possession of other gods *before* God. It does not lay a hand on the Israelites in order to enlighten them that their god is the only god. One ought not to confuse the uniqueness of a highest principle of all things (even when that principle is called by the name of God, that uniqueness about which people can be enlightened if need be) with the uniqueness of God as it is revealed here. It is precisely that unity, be it called the highest being or the absolute spirit or even God, about which people can be enlightened if necessary, which would be one of the other gods which the commandment prohibits us from having before God.

The commandment does not state simply that those other gods have no reality. On the contrary, it assumes that they do have a definite reality just as it assumes that there are peoples who *have* them as gods, who give their *hearts* to them. Precisely where that occurs *there are* gods.

The commandment lays its hand on the Israelites. It isolates all of Israel from those people who have other gods. It demands that they not have those other gods, despite their existence *also* as gods. It demands that they not think of them as gods before the god of Israel, the *deus ecclesiae*, the "I" who addresses the Israelites as "Thou," before the god who led Israel out of Egypt. The Israelites are not to *divide* their hearts between their god and those other gods. "Do not bow down to them and serve them," as it says later. The revelation of God's uniqueness in the first commandment is not a theorem. It is the emergence of *one* god, the *deus ecclesiae* out of the multiplicity of gods (a multiplicity which is initially acknowledged as genuinely indisputable) and this god's reaching out for definite human beings: *I* am your god, and *because* I am your god, I can and will be god *alone*. In this exclusive lordlike act to those people, in this singular conduct, this god exists. God reveals himself as the sole god. God reveals all other gods as nothings. Their reality fades away before God's revelation. Only in giving God and God alone fear, love and confidence do those people know God as the sole god and all other gods as nothings, despite their reality.

We are concerned with a specific and small part of the meaning of this commandment: its meaning for theology. Theology is the attempt, undertaken by the means of human thought and language, to answer scientifically the question of the basis and law of the church and its preaching. By nature theology belongs to the sphere of Holy Scripture and thus to the sphere of the first commandment. Where axioms have their place in other sciences, in theology, prior to any theological thought or speech, there stands as its foundation and criterion (as we have seen, a very different foundation and criterion than all other axioms) the commandment "You shall have no other gods before me!" I think and speak with theological responsibility when I know myself to be responsible to that commandment in what I think and speak as a theologian; when I perceive that responsibility as a responsibility to an authority above which there is no appeal, because it is itself the last and highest, the absolutely decisive authority. "You shall have no other gods before me!"

Nothing is less obvious than the notion that even theology has no other gods before the *deus ecclesiae*! It is as little evident today as it was at Mount Sinai or on the morning when Christ rose from the dead that this god arises and makes it known that "I am the Lord your god!," that God makes other gods into nothings and that he so captures our hearts that we must fear *God*, love *God*, trust *God*. Theology (even theology!) is continually asked where its heart, its concern and interest really lie, and whether its heart might not be divided secretly between this god and the other gods. It is asked, for example, about the concept of the highest *good* or highest *value* presupposed in its work. It is asked about the *source* from which it deduces its statements. It it asked about the standard of *certainty* which it attributes to those statements. It is asked about the practical *motive*, the *intention* according to which it phrases those precise statements in that precise manner. It is asked where it really comes from and where it really is going. And on every side other gods, other grounds and objects of fear, love and trust beside the *deus ecclesiae* are seriously in the running, even and especially for theology.

Is it really true that theology hangs by as thin a thread as we just maintained; by the written account about the temporal event of the god who is merciful in Jesus Christ? Every theology believes and insists that, of course, it "somehow" clings to God. But is it this and only this god, who is revealed here and in that way, the god to whom theology clings? It is here and here only where theology recognizes its highest value, its source of knowledge, its criterion of certainty, its practical motive? One only has to raise this question to understand that in every age theology has sighed and complained about the narrowness of its situation, about the dangerous isolation in which it finds itself and which is so hard to bear, about the questionableness of turning a deaf ear to the voices of the morning, of the beautiful and profound life, of those many other general axioms all around it, which all in their way seem to cry out: *introite nam et hic dii sunt!*

Should God not be greater and richer than that? Should God really be deliniated by the walls of the church, a book, the events of the years 1 to 30, the revelation and faith of the old and New Israel? Poor theology which has so small a god! Poor theology which has to resemble a pyramid standing on its tip! Who can prevent us from asking and complaining that way? Who is to prevent us from asking and complaining that way? Who is to prevent us from searching for help? The word "god" is as passive as all other words. When it comes to this word we are surely at liberty to think polytheistically about *everything* which might appear to us as true, noble and worthy of veneration. Then it might be open to us to promote a corresponding theology according to need and inclination; one oriented towards *this* value and feeding on *that* source, answering the question of certainty *this* way and motivated by *those* practical intentions. A free human being can do all of those things.

That is what recent protestant theology (the theology since the end of the seventeenth and the beginning of the eighteenth centuries) has understood only too well. It thought that it knew better than all earlier theologies that it is really quite difficult to stand so completely alone with God and God's Word (in that narrow, exclusive sense of the word) before philosophy, the historical and natural sciences, and the many other accomplishments of the modern world. More than all other earlier theologies it believed that it had discovered all around itself possibilities and necessities, truths and realities, "concern" and needs. All that it so discovered was so noteworthy, so important, so serious that it was sure that it could not extricate itself from these realities. It was sure it had to give its heart to them and that it had to acknowledge them, for all practical purposes, as a second, third, fourth revelation in addition to the first one.

Thus said the eighteenth century: "Revelation *and* reason." Thus said Schleiermacher: "Revelation *and* religious consciousness." Thus said Ritschl and his disciples: "Revelation *and* ethos of culture." Thus said Troeltsch and his disciples: "Revelation *and* history of religion." Thus it is said in these days from every side: "Revelation *and* creation."

"Revelation *and* primordial revelation." "New Testament *and* human existence." "The commandments *and* the orders of creation."

One must not call into question the freedom to make such discoveries, nor the sincerity, perceptiveness and piety with which and in which they were and still are being made. Nor can one merely arm oneself with the first commandment and note that it was and still is being violated by recent protestant theology. Only the lawgiver himself can and shall be judge about the first commandment and all the others. God alone knows whether a person is willing to give to God his or her heart and whether it is a whole heart or a divided heart. One can only *ask*. One can only ask oneself and the whole of the modern theology of "and" whether there might not be a serious objection against that freedom, against that "and," in view of the responsibility of theology to the first commandment. The following concrete reasons prompt me to raise that question:

1. If theology is aware of its responsibility but deems it necessary to relate the concept of revelation to some other criterion, which for some reason is important, by means of that little but so weighty word "and," then this responsibility will express itself by speaking of revelation with a notably heightened seriousness and interest, and by speaking of that other criterion only secondarily and for the sake of revelation. In the obviously unequal distribution of its zeal and passion, theology will show plainly where its heart is and where it has its god, namely at the point where God, in the commandment, has placed himself. The reformers, as it is well known, did not refuse all recognition to nature, natural theology and natural religion. Nevertheless, it is quite plain where their heart and their god was in their quest for the foundation and law of the church.

In recent protestant theology however, from Buddeus and Pfaff to Hirsch and Althaus, Gogarten and Brunner, it is not clear whether or not their zeal and passion is meant for that other authority. Where does that theology become communicative? Where Angry, happy, emphatic or impressive? Where does it fight its decisive battles? We always hear it speak the loudest, the most urgently and the most solemnly wherever it speaks of those things which have been brought into relation with revelation by means of that little word "and." It began in the eighteenth century with the apology for a certain *petit - bourgeois* morality. Today it seems to end (or indeed does not seem content to end) with the apology for nationhood, morality and the state. Would not the opposite be appropriate, to speak there without emphasis and merely *en passant* as a sign that there are really no "other gods" around, that the heart clings undividedly to the one god?

2. If theology is aware of its responsibility toward the first commandment but, when it speaks of revelation, cannot avoid speaking about humanity, reason and experience, about history and creative existence followed, of course, by nationhood, morality and the state, then this responsibility will express itself by interpreting those other things according to revelation and not the other way round. Theology will not try to illuminate the heavens with a searchlight mounted on earth, but will try to see and understand earth in the light of heaven. I may recall here our earlier attempt to define the axiom of theology. It was done, not on the basis of the general meaning of an axiom, but on the basis of the divine command in its structure of being unconditionally prescribed to us.

Again when it comes to the reformers, we can be sure that, despite their occasional and incidental ventures into natural theology, they "had no other gods." That is, reason, nature and history are not permitted to judge revelation at any important point. The opposite holds true consistently.

One cannot be quite so sure about this in recent Protestant theology. Of what help are the strongest and so very honest assurances of the splendid, even unique significance of biblical revelation when that uniqueness has already been called into question by the method of interpreting that revelation? Has not this theology from the beginning, in its understanding of revelation, by its use of reason, created an example of the control of revelation by reason? Ultimately has it not made of reason a framework, a schema, a criteria by which alone it is able to recognize that revelation as revelation? Is it not true that for Kant, the name of God was *allowed* to say only what it *could* say on the basis of the understanding, and absolutely no more? In every circumstance it had to be an idea of the practical reason. Is it not true that for Schleiermacher, Christ had to be understood solely in the independently discovered dimension of "religion"?

Today is it not the criteria of primordial revelation, orders of creation, human existence (criteria which naturally must be determined beforehand) which individually or together give us the concept, the basis and the system for the theological teaching of the second and third article? Which law is urged on us these days as "pedagogue to Christ"?

The law of Sinai? The law by which nature is at one with the gospel? The law which leads to *Christ* because it *comes* from Christ? Or is it another one, perhaps gleaned from the constitution of the Greek *polis*, of an African tribe or from the ideology of the German Middle Ages? Is it perhaps one gained in the free contemplation of existence and the determination of human nature? After all these teachings, naturally undertaken, will it be the gospel which finally and ultimately gets a hearing? If that is problematical, to some extent at least (despite some very fortunate and praiseworthy inconsistencies), must one not ask whether something like "other gods" beside the *deus ecclesia* has not been allowed into the discussion?

3. If theology, aware of its responsibility to the first commandment, sees revelation in relation (and in its thinking and speaking places in relation — as it *must!*) to reason, existence, creation, or whatever the other criterion is called, then this responsibility will express itself by permitting no possibility (however it is seen and understood) of intermixing, exchanging or identifying the two concepts in this relation.

Calvin, in speaking of the *semen religionis* in the heathen, etc. (*Institutes*, I, 1-5), could have spoken ten times as extensively and emphatically than he actually did. Still, we can be confident that with him there would be *no* reversal of the natural "down here" with the "up there" of grace, predestination, the Word of God and the Holy Spirit, faith, etc.. He has, in fact, "no other gods" in the possibilities and realities which he does not deny, even to fallen humanity. His heart does *not* belong to them. He will *not* consider an apology for other concerns *over against* the concern of the church. He will not consider, therefore, another task of theology. With this reason, justification and faith remain in *their* place just as the gifts of natural humanity remain in *theirs*. Of course, there is no need to add that Luther is just as clear here.

In Protestant theology since 1700, however, everything has begun to swing and sway. Did not the discussion of the eighteenth century and with Wegschneider and company (understanding and misunderstanding the great Kant) happily allow revelation to be absorbed in reason and declare reason itself to be genuine revelation? For Schleiermacher, is revelation more than a determination of the pious self-consciousness? For the theologians of Hegel's school, is revelation more than a part of the absolute spirit's self-progression? Does it not disappear in culture with Ritschl, in the general history of religion and spirit with Troeltsch and his followers, in the conscience with Holl and Hirsch, and in a particular understanding of human existence with Bultmann? Vis-a-vis Brunner and Gogarten I have to ask whether "God" is really more than another word for "neighbour"? Is "commandment" more than another word for the orders of creation? Is "justification" more than another word for life in those orders? And vis-a-vis Bultmann: Are theology and anthropology really interchangeable concepts?

Whenever theology has seriously operated with the arbitrary concept of a special primary revelation derived from creation by means of some more or less intelligent exegesis of our existence, the consequence has always been that *the* revelation of which the *first commandment* speaks has been reduced to something subordinate, a mere shadow. I am really at a loss to interpret differently what I read in Gogarten's book *Ich glaube and den dreieinigen Gott* or in Brunner's ethics about justification. No matter how strenuous the insistence that those orders are to be regarded as the revelation of the sole God, one may well ask whether that would be possible unless there were, in fact, rather mighty, domineering and, in their own way, exclusive "other gods" present in those alleged orders of creation. Yet we hear from all sides that is not how it is meant! Why, then, do they always speak and write those very weighty books as if they did mean it that way?

The question which the first commandment as an axiom of theology makes unavoidable to recent Protestant theology is awesome. It is awesome because the development of that theology (should the question about the "other gods" not be answerable with a decisive "No") would indicate that it has become a very much weaker and unprotected counter image to *that* theology from which the *reformers*, by appealing precisely to the first commandment, *separated* themselves. The reformation became unavoidable because the question whether "other gods" did not influence and seek recognition in the life and teaching of the catholic church, had become urgent and pressing. The catholic church did not part at all with the *deus ecclesiae*. It does know *also* of Christ, *also* of grace, *also* of faith. But it is great in the art of dividing its heart between God and the gods. Alongside Christ it knows of a second thing needful for salvation. It knows of a "down here" which in its existence and actuality is analogous to that "up there" and is oriented toward it in its immanent structures. It knows of humanity and of our capacity to cooperate with grace because of grace, to the glory of God and our own salvation.

In spite of the clever and careful manner in which another authority alongside revelation was validated here, the reformers felt compelled by the first commandment to protest. To God on high *alone* be glory! But the manner in which recent Protestant theology validates other authorities alongside revelation is neither clever nor careful. Compared to its Augustinian and Thomistic counter image it offers a more obvious reason to ask the same question which once led as far as a division of the church. But that is not what makes it awesome for us. That is the question whether theology is in a position to distinguish itself *fundamentally* from its Augustinian - Thomistic counter image or whether this counter image is not indeed its original image, whether it might be no more than a feeble variant of the catholic theme.

I do not say that it is so. Whoever wants to say that would have to move from an *intra*-ecclesial-theological protest to one which would *divide* the church. The question of this intra-ecclesial protest (especially today in the complete darkening of the theological situation which the last years have brought about, mainly in the staggering statements by Bultmann, Brunner and Gogarten) must be registered with more emphasis than ever before. Many roads lead back to Rome!

But that must not be our last word. The fight against natural theology, which is unavoidable in view of the first commandment as an axiom of theology, is a fight for right obedience in theology. Right obedience, the good work of theology, must consist in right theological thought and speech. Theology is right and good when it corresponds to the first commandment and does not oppose it. Even theology has good reason to examine "what is the will of God, what is good and acceptable and perfect" (Romans 12.2). Such an examination leads us to conclude that theology today (and after 400 and especially after 200 years, we today should know what is involved here better than the reformers) should take its leave of each and every natural theology and dare, in that narrow isolation, to cling solely to the god who has revealed himself in Jesus Christ. Why? Because that and only that has been commanded of it. Because everything else is arbitrariness which does not lead to, but leads away from, that god. That is the simple meaning of the thesis which is defended here.

Nevertheless, theology is never justified by what it intends to think and say as its work of right obedience, as fulfillment of the law, according to its best knowledge and conscience. There are no exceptions! Every theology has "other gods" as well, most of all where they are least expected and least noticed. That is why there must be assertion and counter assertion. That is why there must be opposition in theology so that nowhere is there peace with the "other gods" who are also acknowledged and who also exercise control. Even the theology which is oriented very strictly to the first commandment will have cause to remain open to opposition raised against it, perhaps precisely on the basis of the first commandment. Even this theology will never be justified by its work but only, if at all, by the forgiveness of sin.

For that reason the fight in theology — the good and needful fight, the serious fight against Catholicism and the even more serious fight against natural theology in modern Protestantism — can be fought only with a penultimate, never an absolute, seriousness and anger. We cannot see through any theology so completely that we can assert with final certainty that next to the *deus ecclesiae* it has "other gods." We can only remind ourselves mutually of the first commandment. We can only ask. We can only protest when it appears to us that once again the clarity of the relation of theology to the first commandment has been threatened. Nevertheless when we have said everything that has to be said, the "bond of peace" (Ephesians 4.3) must also become visible: the knowledge of the plainly superior wisdom of the *Lord* of the church, the promise "Lo, I am with you always" which we, if we apply it to ourselves, can apply to others no less than to ourselves. The necessary fight of theology can be fought properly only in a common hope. For the present time, that should be the ultimate thing that we must allow ourselves to be taught, precisely by the first commandment.

PHILOSOPHY AND THEOLOGY
By Karl Barth

The opposition of "philosophy" and "theology" is an (slightly mythologizing) abstraction. The reality, meant by that, is the opposition of certain different interested, committed, and occupied *human beings*: the confrontation and cooperation of the philosopher and the theologian. Their confrontation is, in any case, so far also a cooperation, as the difficult tasks of their inquiry and teaching deal with the very same things, but exactly — and that turns their cooperation into a confrontation — in the opposite order and sequence. The philosopher himself will also in the execution of his work have to set forth somewhere and somehow that difficult task which is primary for the theologian, except that in view of his own primary difficult task it does not at present even appear to be a difficult task. And thus will the theologian also have to consider from his perspective and in his way that difficult task which is primary for the philosopher, except that in view of his own primary difficult task it cannot at present yet be or become a difficult task. On the question of the *primacy* of the difficult tasks, as such common to them, their paths themselves separate, they themselves branch off and crisscross significantly and momentously enough. However, during the time that neither of them can simply withdraw himself from the other's pressing difficult task, and during the time that it is still "only" a question as to which difficult task has primacy for the one and which for the other, regarding which their paths separate, they are and remain together as fellow-human beings. The philosopher, who would only know himself to be distant from the theologian, in whose difficult task he is uninterested, would in any case in this respect have to be an inhuman creature and would then certainly also not be a good philosopher. Corresponding to this would be to speak of a theologian, who would let the philosopher's preferred difficult task simply to drop: "pure" theology would be just as inhuman an undertaking as "pure" philosophy. The seriousness of the decision made on both sides and its subsequent separation can do no damage, if on both sides they remain conscious of their humanity — and of this as well, that under all circumstances humanity really signifies *fellow-humanity*. — From that follows first of all two points:

1. The philosopher and the theologian may and should, as each for himself so also each for the other, retain confrontation with the one, single, and whole Truth among all the differentiation of its components: for in having put forward a claim by means of the one, single, whole Truth and therefore reliable, certain ground, object, and content of that active knowledge, in that the human being has been determined and called to be a human being. Not the Truth therefore revealing itself through a double truth, neither through a half truth or only ever through a half configuration! To be a human being means: to be confronted with the one whole Truth disclosing itself in its wholeness. And to be a fellow-human being of a fellow-human being means: to be just in this confrontation responsible with him, his jointly responsible companion, comrade, and colleague. Therewith is the sphere designated, in which the philosopher and the theologian, with regard to the primacy of their common difficult tasks, execute their decisions and their separation, in order to go from there and to set out in earnest upon their different paths. Their separation ensues in the face of the one whole Truth and with the presupposition, that not only the one but also the other may have in view, ponder, and declare just that Truth. Both of their enterprises, on their paths separating themselves on the question of the primacy of their common difficult tasks, will themselves not only have to execute their respective tasks always strictly on the basis of the one whole Truth as such, but also on the basis of the validity of the presupposition that each on its respective path may ever circumnavigate this Truth and only it. More than this is firstly and finally to be demanded neither from the philosopher nor from the theologian. But this is to be demanded of both of them. And that which is to be demanded of both of them includes in itself, that the counting on an immortalizing of their inevitable conflict — which would take the form of an endless "discussion" — is forbidden to them both. As fellow-human beings responsible to the one whole Truth, they have to settle their conflict in all its seriousness — but also in the full hope, which has been given and offered to them throughout the sphere in which the conflict arises and is to be settled.

2. That certain elevated speech in which the philosopher, and that kerygmatic forcefulness with which the theologian will as a rule express himself, changes nothing, viz., that neither the one nor the other is in a position to speak down from heaven thither before himself or with the other. As human beings they have both confronted the one whole

Truth, and it is as human beings that they may both actually circumnavigate this Truth and only it, in this way it is and remains nevertheless for both of them to reflect upon it, thus has neither of them yet the power, as a possessor of it, to lead it into the arena, there to let it speak in behalf of his own subject matter and against that of the other. They can and should indeed let themselves both put forward a claim by means of it, but they cannot lay claim to it for themselves, neither the philosopher nor the theologian. They can both only be at its disposal, viz., to want to serve it. This now signifies again that, in view of the necessary separation and crisscrossing of their ways, the inevitable conflict of their thought and speech, and the "dispute of the faculties" about the primacy of the one or of the other of their common difficult tasks: it is no doubt the case, that the philosopher just as the theologian have ever to conduct the dispute in his own particular way, in order to decide a matter. While they accomplish this, there will indeed be one way according to the philosopher, and another way according to the theologian. In the thought and speech of the one here and of the other there it will therefore certainly be decided, whether it may be the philosopher who "lifts up" the theologian, or the theologian who "lifts up" the philosopher, whether philosophy does the same to theology, or theology does the same to philosophy, to say with Kant, whether in the capacity of "its handmaid it carries the torch in front or carries the train behind." But there can be no talk, where they are both able to carry out this decision only on the earth and as human beings — both in view of the one whole Truth, but both without being able to master it, of singling out one among them, of a fulfilled victory and triumph of either in his relation to the other, of a disposing of the theologian by the philosopher or of the philosopher by the theologian. They both can only appeal to the one whole Truth superior to them both. They both can only run the risk, that this Truth may speak for its own self and may pass judgment on the inevitable dispute between them — perhaps to the surprise and shame of them both. They will, if they are about their proper business, not be permitted to abstain from conducting this "dispute," and to conduct that resolutely and consistently. They will be able to conduct it again from both sides only in great humility and also only with a final sense of humor.

Among the "difficult tasks," about the precedence of which the philosopher as well as the theologian have ever "to dispute" between themselves, but also necessarily among themselves, may be understood the both great seriously opposed but also inseparable successively related components, which the philosopher as well as the theologian deem fitting to perceive as components of the one whole Truth and to have to declare as true, and thereby rightly to be said to become their responsibility in relation to it. With both components of the one whole Truth they both have to do. With both difficult tasks they are both occupied, but exactly in the reverse order — and here arises the dispute.

To the theologian, who speaks here, it has been granted and commanded, that he believes himself to be obliged towards the designation of both of the components of Truth, therefore in what way he also ought to see and declare them, and also both of the difficult tasks, in the undertaking of which he also has endeavored to fulfill sufficiently his responsibility in the face of the one whole Truth, drawing upon one of his own responsibilities, theological language, to serve conceptual pairs, sharply distinguishing and precisely connecting at the same time. He focuses in the one whole Truth on the living *Creator*, establishing in his Word and work the creation, reconciling it with himself, and redeeming it towards full community in life with him. And he focuses in the same, one, whole Truth on the *creation*, established through the Word and work of this its Creator, reconciled with him, and by him being redeemed. To formulate it more briefly and pregnantly: he focuses on the freedom of *God* for his *human being*. And he focuses on the freedom for him given to the two components of truth, he hears the history of philosophy also express loudly these things. With the two corresponding difficult tasks — somewhat complicated certainly by the multiplicity of philosophies — he finds the philosopher also occupied. The matter of idea and appearance, the *causa prima* [primary cause] and those *causae secundae* [secondary causes] moved by it, the "thing in itself" and its theoretical-practical apperception, the *logos* [word] and reason, the spirit and its self-development, transcendence (perhaps also essence) and existence, being and existence, — signified in that way or similarly, conceptual pairs, sharply distinguishing and precisely connecting at the same time, appear also to be situated in the inquiry and doctrine as well as the discussion of the philosopher. And at least something like an analogy of endeavors intrudes here and there. Already certainly the question itself arises: whether they themselves as such prove true — whether with the one theological and the many philosophical conceptual pairs (or at least with one or another among these) both the same components of the one whole Truth may really be designated? Whether the philosopher will be able and inclined to recognize his own contrasts and combinations in the relation of "Creator" and "creation," of "God" and "human being," stated and depicted by the theologian? And whether the theologian on his side will find again in the conceptual pairs of the philosopher that which he understands by "Creator" and "creation," by "God" and "human being?" Whether one here on both sides could with a good conscience come to an understanding thereon, that one indeed may mean and may wish to say "the same thing on this earth?" Whether it also may be opportune or without exception entirely feasible, that the philosopher speaks in the language of the theologian or the theologian in that of the philosopher? It may be, as is well known it has indeed been attempted enough by both. The undertaking is not harmless. The question of vocabulary is already insignificant, if on both sides one knows what one wants to say, since one must say it, surely not to accept that. Could it not be, where it comes to such a mutual recognition, that one on either or both sides has forgotten, perhaps he wanted to forget and also to deny what here just as there was the proper meaning and intention? But one does not forget, how it is said to come then to an acknowledgment also of only an analogical equivalence of the words and concepts used differently by both sides, as under a concealed presupposition: *must it be* "properly" philosophical, or *must it be* "properly" theological, — but *may it be* that at the worst they are also used "improperly," viz., they are thought and spoken by the philosopher theologically, or by the theologian philosophically? Has one himself then understood reciprocally? Can one then hold out for a united ground? Could it not be just in the attempt to interpret the different words and concepts of the other in *meliorem partem* [according to the better part], viz., after the manner of his own measure, and with such an interpretation to adopt them, that the philosopher or theologian is ever more honestly and accurately pushed ahead, until it comes to light that it is not feasible, that on that basis one does not after all mean and intend to say the same thing? For all that, the ideal case is not unthinkable — it could come to be as well as in the inner discussion of the philosopher in company with that which also occupies him theologically, as in that of the theologian for whom the philosophical disposition is also not alien, as finally in the event of their meeting among themselves: that one in the consciousness of the secret taking in of the one by the other, in the absence of which there would thereby be no going astray at least on one side, while one himself would put up with this once again mutually (just secretly or also openly), he may at least come to an understanding concerning an analogical equivalence of the words and concepts used on both sides. The "dispute about words" as such may be peaceful, it may perhaps be settled in a way not tedious, not infruitful, who knows, in a way instructive for both sides. In the "dispute about words" the "dispute of the faculties" used as such, it is not necessary to remain stuck.

Another issue once again situated between the philosopher and the theologian has to do with deciding about the question facing them both as regards the *order* of the components of the one Truth declared by both of them, and also the order of the difficult tasks occupying them both. Here the situation becomes critical, indeed sinister. Here the perspective on a settlement of the dispute — while it here could also as a dispute about the words acquire a new weighty accent — could become very gloomy. An exclusion of one difficult task by the other comes from neither side in question. There is involved on both sides precisely the issue of the *primacy* of the one difficult task before the other, about their *sequence*, viz., once again therefore, the issue as to which of the two includes the other in itself, or the opposite, may be included in the other.

Their earlier indicated formulation was — not only in the choice of words and concepts, but above all in the inconcealable characterization of their relation to each other — no philosophical, also no neutral, but a characteristically theological formulation. The latter circumscribed both difficult tasks in the presupposition, that there is involved here a wholly determined, irreversible priority and posteriority, transcendence and immanence. And the formulation was put in the descending order asserted therewith. There was shown and pondered the descending order from the living Creator here to the living creation over there, from the Word and work of the Creator here on to the determination of his creation founded by him over there, and from divine freedom here to human freedom over there. On the strength of that, then certainly at once and more than ever also the reverse: in the direction away from the creation, from the free human being here back to his Creator over there, to the free God — but yet first thereupon, in a counter-movement from below to above, which becomes possible and real as motivated wholly by the power of the primordial movement from above to below. The theologian stands and falls with this sequence, in fact, with its irreversibility. With every attempt to reverse that sequence, pseudo-theology would begin. To the theologian, who is and remains about his proper business, the one whole Truth in both of its components stands thus and not differently, and he has to declare it thus and not differently. A mighty act of condescension, which as such involves and entails an empowered act of elevation — or to turn it around: an empowered act of elevation, which is enclosed and founded in a mighty act of condescension: this is the Truth, to which the theologian is committed in his thought and speech. Whether he could really declare it just as well in a language different from that expressed will be doubtful. It could indeed also be that his vocabulary stipulates through the prescribed order his thought and speech — it could indeed be that by the order, in which the Truth itself addresses and binds him, that it is forbidden to him to equalize and interchange such concepts as "Creator" and "creation," "God" and "human being," which already as such point to that order and its dynamics, whose content as far as clarity in this respect at least leaves more to be desired. With regard to the *sequence* of both of the components of Truth and of the difficult tasks posited by them, he will again under no circumstances and on no account waver or be able to give ground.

Should it be said that he provides a *philosophia christiana* [Christian philosophy] — as a Christian philosopher, who by the use of another vocabulary would actually also in that order and sequence want to think and speak, while the one whole Truth would actually confront him also thus and not otherwise, while he actually would also have been instructed thereby, to declare it thus and not otherwise? Why should it be said that such a philosopher is not possible? Will one not in any case, in view of the history of philosophy *post Christum natum* [after the birth of Christ] — somewhat boldly perhaps — dare to ask: whether a different Christian philosophy, as one that is at least troubled, disturbed, and somewhat alarmed by the irreversible direction of theological thought and speech, whether in this weaker sense a "Christian" philosophy is generally possible? Whether it *post Christum natum* [after the birth of Christ] exists not also in its "decidedly non-Christian" forms, secretly or at least openly, from its antithesis to the phenomenon of theological thought and speech alien to it? Should it be said that certainly in the existence of a philosophically interested, committed, and preoccupied human being there is a "Christian" philosophy in a strong sense, that is to say, wherein it becomes apparent that he for his part works seriously with the sequence and order of thought and speech offered the theologian — what then would remain over, than to leave to him the responsibility for the vocabulary used by him, in what remains but to address him as a — crypto-theologian?

We fasten on this possibility, thus to set out first of all with the question: whether the theologian indeed perceives and understands the undertaking of the philosopher, if he is of the opinion, that it may proceed now yet — and this also in the era *post Christum natum* [after the birth of Christ], also there, where by means of theological thought and speech it has at least a voice in the decision — in an astounding manner in the direction, which is precisely opposed to that with which he as a theologian stands and falls? The theologian cannot speak for the philosopher, neither can he decide and speak with final certainty on the question of the correctness or incorrectness of his view and understanding of the philosopher. He only can and must say, that he believes that he has to see and to understand him in view of the hitherto existing history of philosophy known to him in this way — in that opposition to his own endeavor. He indeed does not overlook, that the movement from above to below which for him is unconditional and primary is also as such not unfamiliar to the philosopher. But he intends to see, that the movement governing and characterizing the whole, in the thought and speech of the philosopher is honestly not primary, but is secondary, his primary movement being against that, which for him, the theologian, can only be that passing counter-movement from below towards that above. He perceives the philosopher, among the varied previous indications and headings, to be engaged in a mighty elevation — perhaps upwards from the appearance to the idea, from existence to being, from reason to the *logos* [word], from existence to transcendence — always under the presupposition and with the affirmation, or at least suggestion, that for him in that first term of the above pairs in one way or another the second is already included, and also in the interpretation of that first term it may be necessary to consider and unfold the second — in order then in the empowered condescension through the elevation to that second term to revert back to what is for him the first term. The theologian sees the philosopher (expressed in his own theological language, insofar as there could be said to be between the latter and the language of the philosopher thus something like an analogical equivalence to reckon with) on the path from the creation to the Creator, from the human being to God, and from there back again to his own kind of starting-point, to the object (now also still bathed in light with a splendor from above) of his primary interest, viz., to the creation, to the human being. Thus parts the path itself of the philosopher from his own. Precisely this path of the philosopher — has the theologian rightly perceived and understood it? The theologian himself dare not and can not, without becoming a pseudo-theologian, accompany the philosopher and at the same time deem it fitting to remark that the philosopher is ever so little able and willing to accompany him on his theological path — should the latter not be said to be a crypto-theologian, for the latter path the philosopher has left probably only a sympathetic disapproval and smile. It may be asked whether the philosopher in the denotation of his starting-point is already on that account also thus entirely different, that is to say, he must choose such conceptual pairs, which as far as clarity with regard to the question of order are so far inferior to the conceptual pair "Creator and creation" or "God and human being": words, in the interpretation of which the establishment of the order favored by him could not possibly be more distant, yet indeed is the philosopher perhaps lying closer to the theologian? Be that as it may, the theologian believes in the face of the undertaking of the philosopher (the error of whose intention is to be kept in reserve!) to have an occasion for astonishment: on this point, that the latter evidently considers himself free and sees himself in a position to think and speak in view of both of the components of the one whole Truth so completely differently than the theologian himself.

It may be asked whether the decision and separation occuring at this point is just as essential, self-evident, and irrevocably necessary for the philosopher as it is for the theologian? The theologian can here likewise only speak for himself: concerning everything he can listen to reason — but at this point there is for him really no alternative, no deliberation, no discussion, no concession. The question as regards the rank, the order, and the sequence of the difficult tasks has for him been answered, during the time that it has been put. He can describe and explain his path, he can also give an account concerning the point out from which he enters upon his path, but only with the stipulation, that for him it can only be the latter, any other point is once again altogether out of the question. That the dominant difficult task of that thought and speech favored by the philosopher, as he intends to perceive it (he understands it as the difficult task of the creation in view of its Creator), is also not foreign to the theologian, that the latter has to assume this difficult task in his own bailiwick and has to honor it, does not mean that he for his part would likewise have merely the possibility to give to it the priority. He has no *facultas* [capability] to that end. He can only wonder that the philosopher appears to have a *facultas* [capability], the possibility, to think and to speak in this opposite direction. He could also not equally well be a philosopher, much less then, that he as a theologian could be a crypto-philosopher. There is involved here something like a blazing sword, which cuts him off from the path of the philosopher. The path of the philosopher can for the theologian (in that dispute also taking place in his very own self) really only be for him a rejected temptation. Is the philosopher for his own part different in this regard? It is not becoming to the theologian to consider that. But he *does* take a position regarding that. And it is this which makes the antithesis between the philosopher and the theologian critical, indeed sinister. It is certainly no unlimited antithesis. We remind ourselves: it arises and persists in the sphere of the one whole Truth illuminating and surpassing them both, which as such is the hope of them both, and is also the great hope beyond their dispute. But there is within this boundary a dispute, in which there — in any case seen by the theologian here, proceeds a dispute willy-nilly, in which really there can be given no quarter. How shall a thought and speech which — I am again formulating it theologically — begins with creation and humanity as the supposition, elevates itself from there on to the Creator, to God, in order to return from there back to its starting-point, to the creation, to humanity, be said to be reconciled with another for which the Word and work of the Creator is the supposition and also the starting-point, from which it descends to the creation, in order to come again in the Word and work of the Creator to its objective? Are not obviously two distinct lords served here? How can it be said that both these enterprises lead towards one denominator? How can the legitimacy of the one be said to be able to exist beside that of the other? This is indeed the case, that precisely the question of truth, which is put to them both, also steps between them in this way, namely, that in any case by the one side it can prove impossible to have acknowledged that there may be the one whole Truth, which may disclose itself just so in the one order and sequence of its components as in the other order and sequence, it may be therefore that their knowledge and declaration are accomplished just as indeed in the direction of the one hand of a clock moving towards the right as in the direction of the other moving towards the left. There is a painful admission to be made: there is an antithesis, in which in any case by one — the theological — side (always within the known boundary) there can really be no talk of "tolerance." But as a mitigating reminder: "intolerance" may really also on the other side scarcely be avoided and actually-practically may be practiced also often and emphatically enough! Is it not also the case when the philosophers are among themselves?

Invited to give an account on this point, whence the spirit, who leads him in some degree of necessity on the path evidently peculiar to him, now properly comes and whether it goes, the philosopher will . . . but no: it must again be left to the philosopher himself to express himself with regard to that. The theologian will again, invited to give the same account, be able to speak only for his own self and will then, without permitting himself to be ashamed of such naiveté, answer directly and without stipulation — not arbitrarily, but have to confess and testify out of conformity to his message: that Jesus Christ is the one whole Truth, through whom the path of his thought and speech has been shown to him just as strictly as the philosophical path has been cut off. Not a Christ-idea, but the Jesus of Nazareth, who lived under Augustus and Tiberius, has died and been raised from the dead, in order to die no more — and this not as a distinguished (perhaps as the most distinguished) "vehicle" or symbol, as the preferred cipher of the Truth, but the latter one as true God and true human being, as the union established by God between himself and the human being — he himself the Truth illuminating the whole world and thus also the philosopher and the theologian! From his existence comes theological thought and speech hither as from its axiom, and it hastens the theologian as towards his *telos* [end]. It is precisely through him, if it is itself faithful, not only partially determined, but simply determined by him alone. Precisely here is the theologian so astonished concerning the philosopher, because he cannot understand that the latter — *post Christum natum* [after the birth of Christ] existing with him in the same situation! — yet always appears to seek, to find, and to walk the path from the human being to God, from creation to the Creator, and to undertake among these or those indications and claims the construction of a hand of a clock moving from the right towards the left, which yet for him also has been antiquated in Jesus Christ. Precisely from here on has the theologian no *facultas* [capability] for participation in that undertaking. He is and sticks at his own business, therefore his whole thinking and reflection have been (pan noēma [every thought] 2. Cor. 10, 5) "taken captive into the obedience of Christ." Therewith it is clear in which direction he is free to think and to speak. For the path of Jesus Christ clearly leads from above to below and from there back towards the above, from the condescension of the Creator to the elevation of the creation and not the reverse. In Jesus Christ the free grace of God summons the gratitude of the human being, and the free gratitude of the human being answers the grace of God, not the reverse! And while Jesus Christ is the indivisible Truth, besides whom there is no other, he has determined the order and sequence of both components of the Truth and therewith the understanding of both of the difficult tasks pertaining to the Truth. This is — to outline here with the greatest brevity — the answer of the theologian to the question: how he may come to that end, to set out on a path, which must guide him in that uncomfortable situation over against the philosopher.

But we turn, according as this climax has been attained and exceeded, back again most quickly to the stipulation, with which it was here begun: that in the ever so different, indeed, opposing thought and speech just as of the philosopher so also of the theologian, we have to make it with the same human (also far too human) thought and speech. Thus on this point there can indeed yet be no serious judgement and separation between both of them, no incompatibility of their paths, no mild or wild astonishment of the one concerning the other to change something, seeing that everything takes place on one and the same plane, on which every still so radical confrontation includes in itself also a cooperation. Considering the entire acuteness and invincibility of their antithesis, how can and should the just as necessary and immense coexistence itself of the philosopher and of the theologian be formed in the human dignity offered to both of them? A few cautious reflections to that end will evidently not be permitted to go unexpressed here.

In the consciousness of the humanity (the fellow-humanity) of their enterprises, the philosopher and the theologian will surely before everything else not permit themselves to be farther apart than within earshot or to lose sight of each other. Their antithesis is evidently to be just so exciting, so as not to be stimulating in the highest degree. The antithesis requires, that they remain mutually present to each other: that the one may bestow to the greatest possible extent its great attention on the undertaking of the other. And also were it only in order thereby to become clear once more thereon, viz., what has been offered and forbidden to the one himself in distinction to the other! But now yet indeed not only to that end, but also in the open co-operation and in this serious respect, viz., a human being cannot reject the fellow-human being behind the endeavor of the other as of his own, without then also endangering his own humanity, provided it is not granted him to combine himself with the other, and provided he himself can and may only just "come to an understanding" with him. But thereon out perhaps yet also for this reason, because the one, perhaps entirely unexpectedly and contrary to his prospectus, may come to learn that this and that actually have positive significance for his own undertaking and to receive it gratefully. How can it be said not to be permitted and commanded, where the presupposition of the one whole Truth is also imperturbably valid, where their paths must themselves separate in addition to their understanding, to reckon with this possibility, that the one may occasionally meet the other in contexts, in which he cannot follow him, actually as "priest of the most high God," to bear towards him just as King Melchizedek brought the bread and wine to Abraham, actually "to bless" him? Where this becomes possible and actual, it will itself always be negotiated around a free, partial, and non-obligatory learning of the one from the other. Indeed, the learning of the one in the presence of the other will never be able to mean this, that he for his part may now cross over to the path of the other, but only this, that he, without becoming unfaithful to his own responsibility, is guided perhaps on a step of his own path through this or that element in the thought and speech of the other somehow towards a longer stride on this his own path. And thus will the one, from whom the other appears to learn something, not be allowed to expect "to be understood" by the learner in his *own* intention; he himself will not thereon be permitted to fret in seeing the other — evidently engaged in what for him is a fruitful misunderstanding — continue on his own path. That is the limitation, which has fixed the learning coming into question here. Within this limitation it is again possible, that the confrontation of the philosopher and of the theologian becomes cooperation and thus practically significant.

What indeed is the philosopher to learn from the theologian in this situation? If it is anything, provided he is disposed to understand, he himself may imbibe through the theologian as an intelligent expositor, credible representative, and convinced messenger, distinct religious tradition, perhaps readily disposed towards the miracle of it. Is it becoming for him to call attention to "religion," its psychology, sociology, and indeed also its ontology — or more to the point: to attention to the necessity, in the cream of his thought and speech, to assign a suitable place and function also to the Church with its concepts "faith" and "revelation"? Differently then than a misunderstanding evidently fruitful for the philosopher, the theologian himself will certainly not be pleased with this — and he himself will not be able to refrain from interrupting it more than ever, to understand and to suppress it himself according to such measure of philosophical appreciation as bestowed upon him. Again quite certainly, he cannot demand of the philosopher that he leap over his own shadow, it can therefore not hinder him, to understand him now precisely in this way, to want positively to do justice to him in the conducting now of his own undertaking exactly in this way. The philosopher does it on his own responsibility. The theologian cannot dictate to him, what he ought to learn from him. Whatever he may have to say to that end, he certainly would be able, if he should for a moment disclose his gloomy heart, to come to the impudent and intolerable demand, that the philosopher would consider the longest occurring purpose of all philosophy, himself to give therefore at best an analysis of its completed history and beyond that perhaps the drawing up of a formalized logic. How should the theologian presume to be seen by the philosopher therewith? He will have to leave it to the philosopher really, to draw out this or that lesson from the fact of his theological existence.

The theologian can here once again only speak for himself, viz., concerning this, what he for his part believes he can and should learn from the philosopher. It can really be granted him to think not only critically, it must be granted him also to think positively, that he sees the philosopher thus go forward fundamentally in that other order and sequence of the difficult tasks, in which in this way a distinguished, in that way a preferred position falls to the creation, and the human being as the point of departure and goal of his movement. The theologian admires (is again sincerely astonished) the fervor and the ethos, in which the philosopher, while he thinks and speaks in that other order, has been devoted precisely to the creation — with its origin in the Creator and with its relation to him, but still the creation! He admires him as a prudent expositor of its self-understanding and self-description, as a speaker of its knowledge, technical, art, and politics, as a priestly steward of the mystery of its elevation and of the consecration of its nature and culture. He admires him — to take up that good, old word, without the ironical accompanying sound which it has more lately received — as the "*worldly*-wise one." He admires the philosopher therefore sincerely, since precisely in his existence as the "worldly-wise one" he, with an impressiveness and with an energy on which basis it may be permissible to esteem his own self in the highest salutary manner, emphasizes the difficult task, which indeed (as of second order importance certainly) must also interest, engage, and occupy the theologian. That God has created and so loved the *world*, that he gave thither his only Son for it, that in him he has reconciled the *world* with himself — Jesus Christ as the light of the *world* — that indeed is to be his theological theme. But he could in his zeal for the Word and work of God as such, exactly this concrete relation of his Word and work, the creaturely partner placed in union with God, the world reconciled in Jesus Christ with God — he could with regard to the "true God," the "true human being," with regard to the freedom of God, his own, and that of his fellow-human being — if not forgotten, thus after all have treated too casually, seen too blurred, thought too little, and reported too pale. What from all this, which primarily excites the philosopher, should secondarily excite the theologian, but not less urgently and seriously? It has perhaps in practice excited him too little. He has perhaps taken the world of nature and of culture, as well as humanitarianism, too little in earnest, has perhaps (in this case absolutely against his own mandate) thought and spoken with pseudo-prophetic passion much too unworldly and inhumanely. The existence of the philosopher may remind him thereon, that he is not to proceed in this way, that according to his own mandate, at the place where it must occur, he can by no means think and speak worldly, naturally, and humanely enough, that he can by no means praise enough the condescension of the Creator to his *creation* and the elevation of the *creation* to its Creator. When shall the theologian — his execution of his primary difficult task may make him, with a view to his secondary difficult task, slightly careless and unkind — not need to have this reminder again and again, not only on one, but on all the stages of his path? The existence of the philosopher may be helpful to him, to awaken and to keep him on the alert in this respect. May the philosopher after all indeed not become for him in connection with this inducement an *advocatus diaboli* [supporter of the devil]: towards which according to the history of theology — the latter is in this respect a history of catastrophes! At all times and up to this day there is thus a powerful temptation to act out of character, to exchange the path from above to below and from the first to the second for the opposite: to become a crypto-philosopher and thus a pseudo-theologian! That the theologian refrain from presenting himself with an allegedly universal and therefore for him also valid ontology, anthropology, psychology, etc., derived from the philosopher, naturally cannot come into question. He has to take up his second difficult task in all its development in his own context and manner. The philosopher should and can be to him again in any case as an *advocatus hominis et mundi* [supporter of the human being and the world] a reminder, to take up his second difficult task energetically and consistently all along the line. The theologian woud not do well, if he would want to overlook and to ignore the philosopher in this his salutary peculiarity and mission (for this reason, that he must retain his starting-point and path instead of the reverse and cannot conform). Does he not know then, if it is Jesus Christ, the light, the Lord and Savior of the world, who wants to call him through the service of the "worldly-wise one" in that determined direction towards that order, and to introduce him to a "learning of God," the latter, strictly speaking, would have to be called (in view of the double difficult task in it) not "theology" but "theo-anthropology"? Has he, here in this instance it is doubtless reckoned to be, not an inducement, being grateful for the existence of the philosopher and therefore for his work, in such a way radically different from that of his own and therefore he can little follow him, to be, to remain, and to become again and again very alert?

It is henceforth not to be expected, that the philosopher will be pleased with the line, which the theologian himself in his existence tries to effect perhaps in this direction, as is the theologian with the assessment which the philosopher appears to give him. The philosopher may want to look upon himself as more than "only" a "worldly-wise one"! He certainly looks upon the theologian for his part to have comprehended him in terms of a misunderstanding of his undertaking, now evidently fruitful for the theologian, if this — the special attention or the created world, for the human being and his nearest and most remote possibilities — is everything, which he believes can and ought to be learned in connection with him. He may certainly in addition want to be seen, understood, accepted, and then also "admired" by the theologian as something deeper and more universal than in the above way. And thus will be the old yet indeed mutual astonishment itself, just while both endeavor to be themselves, to examine everything, and to retain the best — this time the best in the thought and speech of the fellow-human being, once again and more than ever to inform and for the present not to dispose of the other. Both are allowed to notice, that in any case the one looks out openly and honestly for the best of the other within the boundaries of the *ultra posse nemo obligatur* [no one is obligated beyond his ability] — and both are allowed to be of good confidence, that the still better, which the one expects to hear from the other, to become imparted by word of mouth to each one in its way from an entirely different place, may already be imparted — then it should be possible, that both are for the present themselves satisfied with this, whatever, wisely conceded, the one can and wishes to learn from the other, there may then be misgiving, and at that time in spite of everything both coexist in hope.

And philosopher and theologian are not only fellow-human beings, they may much more both with earnestness also be Christians, then they will, in spite of the last mutual reservation, dare to act in the direction indicated in the Word, viz., Psalm 133, 1. The father of the one celebrating his jubilee — to whom this book and thus also this essay is dedicated — and mine was accustomed, on certain occasions and with raised finger, to call the above text to our attention in our youthful days: "See, how fine and lovely it is, when brothers dwell together in unity!"

www.ingramcontent.com/pod-product-compliance
Lightning Source LLC
Chambersburg PA
CBHW050843160426
43192CB00011B/2132